Gotta ♡ Lebanon for the fragrance of gardenia and jasmine

Gotta Love Lebanon
The Family Guidebook

Gotta ♡ Lebanon because there's never a dull moment

Published by Turning Point Books
15th floor, Concorde Building, Dunan Street, Verdun, Beirut, Lebanon
P.O. Box: 14-6613
www.tpbooksonline.com

First edition: September 2012
Author: Joanne Sayad
Editor: Julie Hannouche
Photographer: Tanya Traboulsi
Graphic Designer: Sinan Hallak

Text © Joanne Sayad, 2012
Photos © Tanya Traboulsi, 2012
Graphic Design © Turning Point Books, 2012

All rights reserved.
No part of this publication may be produced or transmitted in any means without the permission of the publisher.
ISBN 978-9953-0-2352-6
Printing: Dots | www.53dots.com

While every effort has been made to ensure the accuracy of the information within this guidebook, neither the author nor the publisher accepts responsibility for any modifications, omissions or errors regarding the information contained herein.

Preface

Whether you are raising a family in Lebanon or just visiting with children, this guidebook is for you. It provides practical information that will help you plan and navigate – in local terms, *debbro halkon* – your way through to successful family outings, activities and celebrations.

You've heard that Lebanon is an ideal place for families. Close-knit, extended family connections and true friendships create communities so desirable to parents that generations have chosen to raise their children here. Plus, the country is small, by the sea and blessed with great weather, culture and history. It is, by all accounts, extraordinarily fun. Making family outings memorable should be easy, but somehow, it's not. The what, where and how get in the way.

This book lists the best places to go and things to see and do with your children, from ancient sites, art classes and nature treks to beaches, summer camps, amusement parks and even birthday party venues. Most are tried and true. Up-to-date, personalized impressions in this book will help take "family fun" beyond wishful thinking and into reality.

Please note that no list is complete, and that new and interesting places pop up every day. By the same token, establishments sometimes close their doors or change management. Also, getting a store owner to provide a street address or commit to opening hours is not as easy as one might think. The uncertainty keeps things interesting.

Beyond being informative, this guidebook adds value with a Coupon Culture section. Helping our loyal readers stretch their family budgets further is yet another way we hope to be useful.

Finally, from our family to yours: *Yalla* – don't miss a thing.

Turning Point Books

Gotta ♡ Lebanon for its startling contrasts

A Word from the Author

"If you can make it there, you're gonna make it anywhere" is a motto I heard growing up in New York City, but then New York is endowed with so much of what it takes to make a child happy: beautiful parks with old trees, vast, free public libraries and great museums, not to mention Radio City Music Hall, the Brooklyn Botanical Gardens and the Bronx Zoo.

Fast forward to Beirut in 1991: as a newlywed eager to start a family, I found myself a world away from my beloved New York. In those days, Beirut was in a post-war funk, still trying to pick itself up and dust itself off. Reconstruction was just a sketch on paper, an idea to be negotiated.

Still, I had my heart set on finding the best Beirut had to offer a young family. One sure thing was that there were great schools offering a trilingual education. But where would my kids play? What would we do on weekends? How would they learn the arts and music? And where the heck were the trees?

My mission became to purvey all those things. With friends in-the-know and kids in tow, I learned to drive a stick shift and navigate the lawless roads, looking for places with no precise address, all the while feigning fearlessness in the face of the kids. Nothing came easily. No electricity? Switch on the generator. No museum program for the kids? Volunteer and start one up. Want the kids to learn Chinese? Work the phones to get enough parents interested. Soon it became evident that despite Lebanon's political shifts, blunders and tsunamis, the city was more than capable of providing a joyful family life: scores of extra-curricular activities, peerless one-on-one instructors, a vibrant cultural life and nature getaways, all built upon a foundation of close, steady family ties.

Life takes us down unexpected paths. Who knew that a motto so closely associated with New York also rings perfectly true in Beirut? "If you can make it there, you're gonna make it anywhere." Take it from me – you've *Gotta Love Lebanon*. There is so much here to discover and I promise this book will help.

Joanne Sayad

Acknowledgements

I would like to thank Charlotte Hamaoui for giving me the opportunity to write this guidebook. It is because of her support, patience and professionalism that *Gotta Love Lebanon* has come to fruition.

Without my editor, Julie Hannouche, this book would have been no more than a diamond in the rough. "Jewels" is a diamond: she's not only a brilliant editor but also a gem of friend. It's a privilege to work with her. The friendship and laughter we have shared along the way are priceless.

Thanks to my dear and longtime friend Sabina Llewellyn-Davies for hooking me up with Turning Point Books and for encouraging me to work. Over the years, Sabina's kindness, inner strength and friendship have been a tremendous blessing.

I also would like to thank graphic designer Sinan Hallak and photographer Tanya Traboulsi for their creative talent.

Cheers to the kind people we reached out to in a last minute scramble for photos: Badeeh Abla, Mary Cochrane, Shawna Zard, Joanne Karkour, Sabi Mahfoud, Eric Ritter and Nour Saab. And to Badria Moghrabi, Eleena Sarkissian and Caterina Belardi for pitching in to double check listings. Your contributions are much appreciated.

Finally, so much depends upon the love and support of my family. They are my life's truest guide.

For Roffo, Jamjoumi, Kiko and Ralph le Kbeer:
Gotta love Lebanon for your nicknames.

Follow the little birdie tweets for interesting and sometimes quirky info...

Table of Contents

018 Arts

038 Culture Vulture

070 Museums & More

094 Public Gardens & Libraries

110 Snow Sensation

130 Nature

152 Summer Camps

168 Beach Bliss

182 Amusing Parks & More

194 Birthday Bling

216 Beirut & Beyond

227 Getting the Gist of Beirut

231 Coupon Culture

"Lebanon is but a canvas for our imagination." **Anonymous**

Arts

IF your cupboard is stocked with colored pencils, glue sticks and construction paper, you'll be glad to know that opportunities for your child to be creative go far beyond the confines of home on a rainy day. Canvas the city and you'll find that every other person, it seems, is either an entrepreneur or an artist, and sometimes both! Since the Phoenicians' wildly successful artistic enterprise known as purple murex dye, the business of creativity has found in Beirut a natural marketplace, and it is thriving. In private ateliers, corner cafés, industrial workshops and everywhere in between, qualified practitioners, some quite accomplished, are inspiring creative sparks in both young and old. There's so much more than painting – ceramics, mosaics, fashion design, the culinary arts, photography and more – if you know where to look.

STUDIOS

Mona Trad Dabaji

American University of Beirut (AUB) graduate and teacher since 1993, this quintessentially Lebanese artist has been attracting international acclaim. Her work includes salvaging architectural woodwork from traditional Lebanese homes, designing tiles, trays and tables and illustrating the children's book, *Lebanon 1-2-3*. She oversees the preparation of portfolios in her charming old studio with soaring ceilings and works on her own canvases as cats roam and music plays. Mona's artist daughter shares the eclectic space, giving lessons to children in the same studio.

🏠 Achrafieh 📞 03-139 313 🌐 www.monatraddabaji.com

Mona Trad Dabaji

Nathalie Khayat Ceramics Studio

An accomplished ceramicist, her recent exhibit at Beirut Art Center showcased organic forms with captured textures and shapes of seeds. Nathalie has a guru following, particularly among women with a refined eye for art and a lifestyle to match. She studied in Montreal, returning to Beirut in 2000 to instruct in the wheel and hand-building methods. Some of her protégées, having begun with local red clay, graduated to imported white faïence then went on to exhibit internationally. Students meet for three hours weekly and look forward to an annual outdoor *raku* firing (a Japanese technique) at the artist's mountain home. There is a waiting list for her classes.

🏠 Achrafieh, Traboulsi Building, Sassine Street 📞 03-751 555
🌐 www.nathaliekhayat.com

Jean-Marc Nahas

A true artist in lifestyle and character, Jean-Marc rides his motorcycle from his mountain home to his Achrafieh studio which has an unmistakable bachelor-pad feel. His work – mostly acrylic on wood and canvas – has become popular with the "in crowd" and is in demand by designers, restaurateurs and gallery owners. When he's not magic markering up restaurant walls, turning furniture into hip sculptural whimsies or decorating a line of limited edition Johnny Farah handbags, he helps serious art students prepare their portfolios. As a professor at l'Académie Libanaise des Beaux-Arts (ALBA), he knows what it takes. As an artist, he does, too: his work is represented in the British Museum.

🏠 Achrafieh 📞 03-608 528 🌐 www.jeanmarcnahas.com

Private Art Studio

Using charcoal and pastel, Raya Mazigi creates strikingly simple compositions, very often with poignant messages. The Lebanese Ministry of Culture recently acquired her work, peace ii-*paper Planes*, and the Sursock's Museum Salon d'Automne as well as galleries abroad have featured her paintings. Raya earned a master's degree in visual arts in Montreal, where she met her artist husband. Together they opened Private Studio and have hired like-minded instructors to help young students find their style through watercolor, acrylic and oil painting.

🏠 Achrafieh, Sassine 📞 70-868 837

Gaby Maamari Atelier

Gaby is an artist, art critic and art historian who loves to practice experimental theater. He's got a PhD from the Sorbonne, 20 years of experience teaching studio arts and is a well-respected professor of art history and the history of architecture at Balamand University. Did we mention he's an author, too, having recently published *Carnet d'Artist*? Luckily for his students (ages 12 and over), he finds time to give drawing and painting lessons.

🏠 Furn el Chebbak, Moudar Street 📞 03-278 042

Atelier Lulu Baassiri

Lulu's canvases are colorful with a splash of brash; she paints in acrylic as well as mixed media using a precise technique so realistic it looks photographic. While at the Lebanese American University (LAU; BUC back in the day), she won a scholarship from the Italian Embassy to study painting in Perugia. Back in Lebanon, she made a career as an art director for Arabic newspapers. For the past eight years she has been teaching at AUB as well as privately from her workspace, using an art therapy-type method to guide students toward their visual style. She teaches students 12 and older in groups of eight or fewer.

Sanayeh, Dhalayni Building   01-737 089   03-855 942

Art Class

American artist from Rhode Island Nancy Salamouny graduated from the University of Massachusetts in 1984 with a degree in fine arts. When she moved to Beirut 18 years ago with her Lebanese husband, she taught art at the school her daughters were attending. A seasoned teacher, Nancy has amassed over 20 years of experience teaching drawing, painting and sculpture to toddlers through teens. Currently art department coordinator for a network of private schools in Beirut, she also takes on private commissions for portraits and wall murals. Nancy just opened a studio and is dedicated to helping students of all ages explore their own creativity.

Achrafieh, Salamouny Building Block 2, Ghandour el Saad Street   70-213 418

SCHOOLS

Ecole des Arts: Ghassan Yammine

Private school for the arts (see also Culture Vulture and Photography). The 4-year-old visual arts program offers instruction in mixed media, acrylic, oil, gouache, aquarelle, wood and wax crayon. Classes meet weekly for an hour and a half. Class size is six maximum. For 5-years and older. All materials are provided.

Sodeco   01-202 820   Hamra   01-350 310   Jal el Dib
04-980 656   Ghazir   09-850 202   Beit Chabab   04-711 047

Toros Roslin Fine Arts School

Finding it is a feat, nestled as it is in ghetto-like environs, but once inside this 30-year-old institution, you know you have arrived by the virtuoso piano playing. Based in the Hamazkayin Armenian and Educational Center in Bourj Hammoud, the school offers painting and sculpture courses taught by accomplished instructors and accepts students as young as five. To study here is to be immersed in a community that values the arts and practices with dedication. A branch in Antelias carries on the tradition.

🏠 Bourj Hammoud, Hamazkayin Art Center ☎ 01-249 375 ☎ 01-265 899
🏠 Antelias, Aghpalian Center ☎ 04-715 491

WORKSHOPS

BEC Workshops for the Young

Aiming with precision at children between the ages of 7 and 12, the Beirut Exhibition Center has devised a series of workshops using the work of local and regional artists as a foundation for teaching theory and practice. Guest appearances by the artists themselves and the study of their actual work distinguishes this program. Workshops run in a cycle of 10 two-hour long sessions.

🏠 Beirut Waterfront ☎ 01-980 650 ext. 2883
🌐 www.beirutexhibitioncenter.com

> This promises to be world class!

The Running Horse Contemporary Art Space

This hip gallery hosts contemporary exhibits for all, and for children, the Running Kids Art Program. It's *the* place for a comprehensive experience: classes begin with a slide show on the history of the art movement in question followed by a hands-on experience related to the theme. Here, children learn to articulate their own responses to the world through the visual language of art. Courses run in a cycle of nine sessions; all materials – even snacks – are provided.

🏠 Karantina, Sleep Comfort Depot Building, Shukri el Khoury Street, Khodr Sector
☎ 01-562 778 📠 03-710 225 🌐 www.therunninghorseart.com

The Artwork Shop

Raised in Manchester, England, Omayma Soubra studied at ALBA and stayed on to establish The Artwork Shop in 1996. Onsite are a café, gallery and shop, where students are welcome to peruse art books and periodicals and consult the in-house events calendar. The course offerings alone are a source of inspiration: from cooking and table etiquette for children to custom jewelry design, it's all about discovering one's own style. Adolescents can choose from fashion design, interior design, sculpture, illustration, and pottery. Adult classes also offered. All materials provided. Walk-ins welcome Saturdays from 11am-1pm. Website lists current curriculum; minimum of five students required per class.

🏠 Hamra, Aayad Building, Adonis Street   ☎ 01-749 646   📱 03-754 867
🌐 www.theartworkshop.net

La Petite Académie

This street-corner boutique with stone arches provides a lovely haven where kids aged 3-16 can come after school and during holidays to learn drawing, painting and sculpture as well as mixed media, crafts and mosaics. The French franchise offers a wide choice of courses, and adults are welcome, too.

🏠 Achrafieh, Haddad Building, Chehade Street
☎ 01-201 353   📱 03-668 071   🌐 www.lapetiteacademie.net

Dana Adada Mosaics

Early in her career, Dana Adada ran mosaic workshops at the Beirut Children's Museum. Today she has a regular gig teaching adults at the University of Saint Joseph's extension program, but she may be best known as the go-to person in Beirut for special commissions. Upon request, she gives private workshops for groups, ages 14 and older, including birthday parties.

🏠 Corniche el Mazraa, Peugeot Building   ☎ 01-660 077   📱 03-234 998
🌐 www.danaadada.com

La Maison des Artistes

An open workshop of sorts, an informal prep school where aspiring artists work seriously alongside a core group of regulars in a roundtable group environment. During hour-long, weekly sessions, participants can prepare portfolios for admission into university art programs or for other specific purposes. Zoha Nassif has administered the sessions since 1999.

Achrafieh, Adib Isaac Street 01-216 905 03-809 009 www.zohanassif.com

Petits Talents

This new workshop, small but furnished adorably with salvaged furniture, radiates a fresh and positive vibe. Director Marie-Joe Ayoub took art lessons at a gallery not far from here as a child; now the illustrator/ALBA graduate offers a distinctive program based on the Betty Edwards' "Right Brain Drawing" method, which is designed to transcend age and ability. The curriculum is for 5-10-year-olds and covers drawing, painting and crafts.

Achrafieh, Toufic Rizk Street 03-541 333 Petits Talents

La Pyramide des Arts

Primarily a painting program following the classic beaux-arts curriculum. Here, students are required to try their hand at all media during two-hour-long sessions held either once or twice per week. Materials are provided during the first month. After ALBA, director Josée Abi Zeid got a degree in painting restoration from City and Guilds of London Institute; in 1997 she opened this apartment workshop. There is a gallery with paintings for sale on the premises.

Gemmayze, Centre Medawar, Pasteur Street 01-562 299 03-290 860

Art 4 Art

Operates in a converted depot at the entrance of an underground parking garage; Nabia Salhab brings to the Spears neighborhood what is basically an arts and crafts center, coordinating work in mosaics, stained glass, candle making, jewelry, decoupage, needlework and more. Painting and photography instruction is also available. Across the street, her boutique sells handmade gifts.

Sanayeh, Zuhour Building, Salim Boustani Street 01-744 989 03-679 280

The Artwork Shop's cookie and cake counter

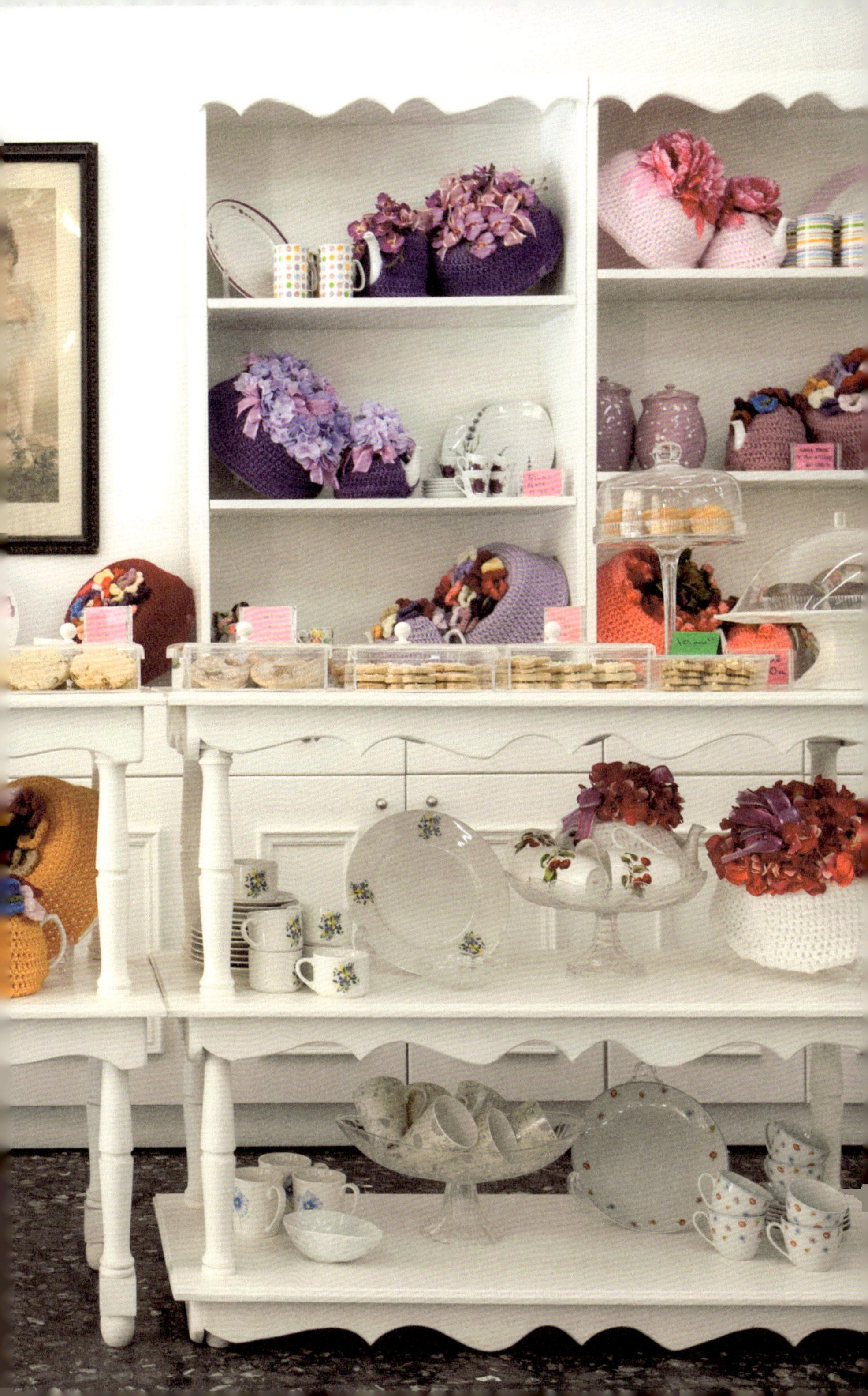

Art'Brico

Geen Damien opened this studio for kids-only (3-16 years) in the summer of 2011, after graduating with a master's degree in fine arts from the Lebanese University and a stint in Australia. From Jackson Pollock-style action painting to classic portraiture, painting and drawing are the focus here, with the exception of Fridays, when it's sculpture in wood or red earth clay. The space can be hired out for events such as birthday parties.

🏠 Jdeideh, Boulos Center, Assaily Street ☎ 01-901 186 📱 71-960 766
🌐 www.artbrico.com ƒ ArtBrico

Eurêka Brain Booster Center

May sound intimidating, but is actually a super friendly and accommodating environment for children. Opened in 2009 by the dynamic, affable and cultured Carmen Salame to provide after-school academic support, the center quickly grew to include the Eurêka Arts Department, which offers courses for all ages in drawing, painting, cooking, mosaics and photography. Sure beats algebra.

🏠 Rabieh 3, Building 593, 28th Street ☎ 04-521 126 📱 70-776 148
🌐 www.eurekabbc.com

Fabriano Art School

Art supplies a-go-go! Fabriano is the renowned Italian art supply brand of the same name. Since 1965, the mother company has sponsored an annual drawing contest for Lebanese students and since 1971 has awarded coveted scholarships to art academies in Italy. At two Lebanese workshops, in Verdun and Zalka, students of all ages learn drawing, acrylic and oil painting, collage and crafts.

🏠 Verdun, Safiaddina Building, Verdun Street ☎ 01-810 159
🏠 Zalka, Abou Ghazali Building ☎ 01-889 809 🌐 www.fabrianolebanon.com

Monart

In 2003, ALBA graduate and former Sainte Famille art teacher Mona Khoury Khabsa established Monart in a beautiful Lebanese ancestral home overlooking the Bay of Jounieh. She teaches the foundations of art to students four years and older through perspective and color theory using media such as charcoal, watercolor, acrylic, gouache and oil pastel. Classes meet weekly for two hours in a cycle of 12 sessions.

🏠 Jounieh, Sabra descent ☎ 09-930 145 📱 70-846 532 ƒ Atelier Monart

> Art runs in the family: in the same house, Mona's daughter teaches dance and her husband creates jewelry.

Arts & Renaissance

Since 1994, Fouad Tomb has been teaching techniques in acrylic, oil, pastel, charcoal, watercolor and mixed media out of a spacious garden apartment. Students aged five and older learn by emulating the styles of famous artists such as Old Masters Renoir and Rembrandt. Fouad's daughter Sandra, an artist in her own right, also teaches at the workshop.

🏠 Kfarhebab, Building 14, V5 Road ☎ 09-921 618 📱 03-327 837
🌐 www.arts-renaissance.com

CRAFTING

Hype 'n' Hop

Activity center with an arts and crafts workstation where children can paint on ceramics, canvas and wood. There's also a cooking club for 5-6 year-olds.

🏠 Ramlet el Baida, Saikaly Building ☎ 01-790 035/36 ⨍ Hype 'n' Hop

L'Univers d'Albert

Play center offering anytime crafting, cooking and wall painting for children 3-9-years-old. Call ahead, because often the place is booked for birthday parties (see Birthday Bling).

🏠 Rabieh, Azar Center, Rabieh Highway ☎ 04-402 823 🌐 www.luniversdalbert.com
⨍ L'univers d'Albert

Oh! happy days

Small, friendly entertainment services boutique (see Birthday Bling) with activities for kids aged 2-10. Puppet shows and crafts are often on the schedule; call ahead to check.

🏠 Achrafieh, Abou Rizk Building, Abdel Wahab el Inglizi Street ☎ 01-215 831
🌐 www.ohhappydayslb.com

Fun Factory

Has two stations within its 1000-square-meter entertainment center where kids can make crafts or get cooking. There's a drawing and ceramic corner, where an assistant oversees small projects and a cooking area with a small oven and tables for turning ingredients into yummy things like cupcakes and cookies.

🏠 Zouk Mosbeh, Joe & Joe Center, Zouk Mosbeh Highway   ☎ 09-217 697

CERAMICS

Trendy ceramic lounges are a great venue for birthday parties!

L'Atelier Art Lounge

You know what they say about location. This brand new ceramic lounge has established itself in glitzy Zaitunay Bay, right on the pedestrian pier on the Marina. This setting gives a kind of good mood/vacation feel to the lounge, which is a well-designed space with great daylight. The set-up of separate art stations is well-thought-out and conducive to creativity. Really nice place for kids and their parents to paint on ceramics, porcelain, fabric, glass, pottery, wood and plaster. In addition, they have mosaic and scrapbook projects. Tiny tots have a special room all their own for wall painting and finger painting. An onsite café serves crepes, coffees, smoothies, milkshakes and more. Throughout the year, the lounge celebrates holidays and birthdays with special, themed events.

🏠 Zaitunay Bay, Beirut Marina   ☎ 01-370 181   🌐 www.latelier-artlounge.com
f atelierartlounge

Ceramics 'N More

This craft workshop/boutique offers a large selection of ceramic bisque pieces for patrons to stencil or sketch their own designs onto. Walk in whenever the mood strikes, select your colors, glaze, and an assistant will kiln-fire your work for you. Pick up the finished product a week later. Opens Monday through Saturday from 10am-10 pm, Sunday afternoons from 2pm-10pm.

🏠 Sodeco Square   ☎ 01-424 516   📱 70-202 723   🌐 www.ceramics-n-more.com

Busy Box Arts and Crafts Lounge

Located beneath the Crowne Plaza hotel in the heart of Hamra, this venue is owned and run by Maha Ayass and Lina Hamadeh, friends who studied pottery for 12 years in Riyadh under an Iranian ceramicist. Staffed with helpful attendants who are also art students, the lounge carries a large selection of wooden, porcelain and ceramic items for decorating. Here kids can pass a creative vacation day or longer making soap, decorating cookies or designing jewelry while grateful parents sip coffee. They say Busy Box is the best place in town for scrapbooking.

Hamra, Taj Tower Center (Crowne Plaza), Hamra Street
01-740 171   03-333 659

Nadine Tawil Abou Atelier and Boutique

Nadine has become known for her artistic, handmade pottery creations, a popular choice for birth, wedding and baptism souvenirs. She is equally successful running four-session workshops for children in which they make pottery from scratch – molding the earth clay themselves. The children's creations are fired and twice glazed in Nadine's home kiln and ready to be retrieved during the next week's session.

Achrafieh, Beydoun Building, Nazareth Street   03-366 000
www.nadineabou.com

L'atelier du Coin

Lena Traboulsi earned street cred as a kindergarten teacher before studying art, a good background for running this arts and crafts workshop for children aged 4-years-old and up. She's converted two rooms of an apartment for studio work and a third for selling her own sentimental creations: painted glass, wood and ceramic. Lena also teaches the basics of drawing and painting and directs craft projects in hour-long weekly sessions (two hours for adults). Private lessons can be arranged.

📍 Achrafieh, El Hajj Building, Alfred Naccache Street ☎ 03-325 006

CULINARY ARTS

Ghazl el Banet

Cooking up a masterpiece is a delightful, delicious activity for kids that can turn into a lifelong creative outlet. Ghazel el Banet means cotton candy, and in this boutique space, located next to the cinema in Sodeco Square, kids can smell and see a cotton candy machine at work. This is no accident, but rather an experience designed to introduce the senses to the store's fun concept of culinary workshops, where kids take hour-long lessons in preparing either a gourmet meal or something less ambitious. The shop is open daily from 10am-7pm; workshops are booked by appointment.

📍 Sodeco Square ☎ 01-426 466

PHOTOGRAPHY

Dar el Mousawwir

House of Photography in English, this center organizes 12 exhibits throughout the year and provides lectures, seminars and photo services. Onsite are a library, photography equipment, studio, dark room and a school, where photography workshops, including digital, analog, Photoshop and video are held. Sessions meet twice a week on a monthly basis and are taught by professionals. Located above a charming book and bistro boutique in a traditional building, there's a bohemian and creative vibe to the place. They keep class size to fewer than 10 and take students from 10-100 years old.

📍 Hamra, Alley 83 off Roma Street, Wardiyeh ☎ 01-373 347 📱 71-236 627
@ Daralmussawir@gmail.com

Nikon School

Launched in 2011 by Nikon's distributor in Lebanon, this organization grants certificates upon completion of their workshops, which start at the beginner's level with Fundamentals of Photography and progress to the advanced, with courses such as Advanced and Post Processing Photo Techniques. Teachers are professional photographers. The official workshop is situated in Jal el Dib but they also arrange for classes to be held in their Hamra offices.

📍 Hamra, Adhami Building, Neemat Yafet Street
☎ 01-738 802 🌐 www.nikon.com.lb

Ecole des Arts: Ghassan Yammine

What began years ago as a music school evolved to include the visual arts, including, as of 2010, photography. During a four-session course designed for amateurs, students explore the art, master technical skills and hone their visual sensibility with the aim of capturing great shots. The comprehensive curriculum includes the effects of different lenses, the performance of exposure and depth of field, quality of light and light temperature, histograms, composition, the usage of flash, the advantages of shooting in the raw vs. JPG as well as the basics of post–processing techniques. Open to ages 15 and older, the program is offered at the school's Hamra and Jal el Dib locations only.

📍 Jal el Dib, Mazda Building, Autostrade ☎ 04-711 047
📍 Hamra, Broadway Center ☎ 01-350 310 🌐 www.edagy.com

FASHION

ESMOD Beirut

Oh, la, la! ESMOD (Ecole Supérieure de Mode) is Lebanon's fashion university. Fashion design, always à la mode in Lebanon, is becoming particularly so for the 12-20 set, who demanded – and received – weekend courses designed especially for them. Kids learn the theory of color combination and put their lessons into practice hand working basic t-shirts which they are encouraged to personalize. Who knows which of them will be the next Elie Saab?

Ain Mreisseh, Roustom Basha Street
01-361 242   03-530 543   www.esmodbeyrouth.com

ESMOD is the alma mater of celebrated Lebanese fashion designer Elie Saab.

Whether your household is brimming with creative impulses or entirely devoid of them, a great family activity is admiring the particular traditions and handiwork of Lebanese artisans: pottery, hand-blown glass, hand-tooled cooper and brassware, embroidery and inlaid mother of pearl as well as the traditional mosaic and bone cutlery that is unique to Jezzine. Here are some top shops for buying ready-made artisanal crafts:

L'Artisan du Liban   Achrafieh   01-580 618   Clemenceau   01-364 880

Orient 499   Minet el Hosn   01-369 499

Maison de L'Artisan   Ain Mreisseh   01-368 488

Finikia   Gemmayze   01-566 867

ART IS FOR EVERYBODY -EXCEPT UGLY PEOPLE

Stencil art grafitti found around Beirut

Art Classes for Adults

Adults can choose from a variety of art classes within the context of continuing education programs at leading Lebanese universities in Beirut.

American University of Beirut

At its Raouché campus, AUB's Continuing Education Center (CEC) arranges a customized curriculum upon request for individuals or groups in life drawing, basic and creative photography and art history.

 www.aub.edu.lb

Haigazian University

The Center for Continuing Studies offers workshops, lectures and courses in drawing, arts and crafts and art appreciation at the Beirut campus.

 www.haigazian.edu.lb

Lebanese American University

LAU's Continuing Education Program (CEP) offers certificate programs in graphic design as well as courses for personal enrichment in painting, drawing, photography, pottery, jewelry, craftsmanship and home decoration. There are two campuses: Beirut and Byblos.

 www.cep.lau.edu

Saint Joseph University

Instruction is in the French language at l'Université Saint-Joseph (USJ) off Rue Monot. Through an extension program called Université Pour Tous, the university offers a great series of workshops in drawing, mosaics, painting and sculpture; all are held in a historic, cathedral-like church.

 www.usj.edu.lb

Painting class at UPT

UPT sculpture studio for adult students

Check out Mouawad Museum's art appreciation classes for adults

> "A nation's culture resides in the hearts and in the soul of its people." **Mahtma Ghandi**

Culture Vulture

For those ravenous for culture, Beirut lives and breathes it! The archaeological vestiges preserved within the city center and the eclectic collection of historical churches and mosques juxtaposed with the contemporary art galleries and performing arts festivals give Beirut a freshness that belies its Byzantine years. Lebanon's pedigree contains the DNA of so many civilizations, from the Phoenician, Assyrian, Persian, Greek, Roman, Arab, Crusader and Ottoman Turk to the current, a French-mandate colony culture that accounts for the city's distinctly sophisticated accent. The Lebanese dialect of Arabic is the official spoken language, but the food, music and literature reflect wider Levantine influences and in many ways resemble the lifestyle and landscape of eastern Mediterranean countries. The happy result is a rich and broad cultural scene in which to revel.

Periodicals to help navigate the buzzing cultural scene:

Agenda Culturel bi-monthly available at newsstands, by subscription or online

Time Out Beirut monthly guide available at newsstands or online

The Daily Star, L'Orient le Jour predominant English and French-language daily papers

Al Nahar, As Safir major Arabic dailies

CULTURAL CENTERS

A polyglot's paradise, Lebanon is one of the few countries in the world that's truly trilingual. Many locals speak Arabic, French and English (famously using all three in one sentence); still, the population is keen to pick up even more languages, and they do so at cultural centers affiliated with foreign embassies. Spanish and Italian are perennial favorites, but the latest craze is Chinese. Giving children the gift of languages is easy here, and an opportunity not to be missed. Giving them an appreciation for different cultures is fun, because all of these centers sponsor fascinating events throughout the year.

British Council

During the academic year, the Council teaches English to adults and offers an official exam preparation course for students planning to study in the UK, Australia, New Zealand, Canada, the US or Europe. Entrance exams, including the Cambridge ESOL and IELTS, are administered here on behalf of British institutions. Runs a summer English-language program for children 10-18 and provides a study room with reference books for all.

Mat-haf, Bertytech Building, Damascus Road 01-428 900
www.britishcouncil.org/lebanon

Institut Français du Liban

Formerly known as the Centre Culturel Français, this is France's cultural mission *par excellence*. Fabulous about preserving and sharing their culture in Lebanon, the French run a first-class French language program and organize exhibits, lectures and conferences throughout the year. The institute houses a wonderful library with an extensive range of books, periodicals, CDs and movies (check out the cine club) for both children and adults. On the landscaped grounds in Beirut there's a popular café/restaurant, perfect for families. Presenting regular exhibitions and book fairs, the institute offers French language certificate courses for all ages and serves as a resource center for studying in France. In Beirut, *l'Institut* is conveniently situated next to the French Embassy but branches are scattered throughout the country, in Baalbek, Deir el Qamar, Jounieh, Nabatieh, Saida, Tripoli and Tyre.

📍 Mat-haf, Damascus Road ☎ 01-420 230 🌐 www.institutfrancais-liban.com

Armenian Cultural Center

Also known as the Levon Shant Cultural Center, this offshoot of the Hamazkayin Armenian Educational and Cultural society runs programs in theatre, arts and music. Their agenda is to preserve the Armenian heritage and keep a connection and exchange with Yerevan.

📍 Bourj Hammoud ☎ 01-249 375 @ lebregcom@hamazkayin.com

Confucius Institute

The fruit of a joint academic cooperation between Saint Joseph University (USJ) and Shenyang Normal University in China, the first Chinese cultural center in Lebanon opened in 2009. Confucius offers Chinese language courses for all ages, hosts cultural activities and sponsors scholarships as well as travel in China.

📍 USJ Humanities Campus (CSH), Damascus Road ☎ 01-421 590

Goethe-Institut

From this well-established base the German culture is propagated through functions and language instruction for adults and children (ages 4-7). Adult language classes are given in cooperation with Collège du Sacré-Cœur in Gemmayze. Goethe has a library and information services for studying in Germany as well as a comprehensive exam program.

🏠 Mat-haf, Bertytech Building, Damascus Road ☎ 01-422 291
🌐 www.goethe.de/beirut

Cervantes

At this center your kids can learn to speak Spanish, to play Spanish guitar and even how to live like a Spaniard in Beirut. Open to the public, the library is stocked with important reference works and volumes of Spanish and Latin American literature plus a large selection of films.

🏠 Beirut, Maarad Street, City Center ☎ 01-970 253/4/5

Italian Cultural Center

Italian language courses for yourself or your *bella bambino*, cooking courses, an extensive library and a cine club are among the many cultural offerings at this center.

🏠 Hamra, Najjar Building, Rome Street ☎ 01-749 801/2/3

Japan Academic Center

Founded in 2008 after a successful exchange between USJ and Japan's Keiko University, the organization offers Japanese language courses using the latest audio visual method, a really great way to learn. Karate and Aikido classes as well.

🏠 USJ Social Sciences Campus, Huvelin Street ☎ 01-421 410 ✉ cajap@usj.edu.lb

Russian Cultural Center

With a history of over 60 years in Beirut, the Russian Cultural Center offers not only language courses for children and adults but also the excellent training for which they are known in classical ballet, piano, gymnastics and many other activities.

🏠 Verdun, Verdun Street ☎ 01-790 907

Brazilian Cultural Center

Housed in a recently restored, three-level traditional Lebanese town house with distinctive burgundy façade, the center is just as alluring inside as out with its programs: Portuguese and spoken Arabic language courses, conferences on Brazilian culture, dance, Jiu-jitsu and gastronomy. There's a projection room for cine club, a library, a café/bar and garden. And yes, you can learn to dance the samba!

Achrafieh, Mar Mitr ☎ 01-322 905 @ centreculturelbresilliban@gmail.com

Saifi Institute for Arabic Language

Set in a picturesque, restored alleyway that connects a series of salvaged, traditional stone buildings overlooking the port of Beirut lies this unique and hip learning center. Foreigners flock here in an attempt to master Arabic in both the colloquial and the written classical form. Studying in an urban garden amidst unusual sculptures can be found an interesting student body, from Harvard scholars, foreign journalists and expats to free-spirited high school students on a summer crash course. Beyond its obvious language draw, the institute offers a rich cultural vibe, organizing as they do lectures and courses such as Arabic calligraphy. What's more is that dorms are reasonably priced, there's a homey mom and pop café/resto serving Lebanese dishes and a roof top bar, Coup d'état, that's authentically bohemian. Learning Arabic doesn't get better than this.

Gemmayze, Saifi Urban Gardens Building, Pasteur Street ☎ 01-560 738
www.saifiarabic.com

Hellenic Club

Just off the port, not of Piraeus, but Beirut, the Hellenic Club promotes cultural exchange, mainly through Greek language courses taught by a government-appointed Greek teacher (due to the debt crisis in effect when this guide went to print, lessons are no longer free). The music lending library is popular with families for discovering Greek composers, singers and the sound of the *bouzouki*. The Friends of Nikos Kazantzakis, a club for fans of *Zorba the Greek*, meets here. *Opa!*

🏠 Beirut, Massoud Building, Charles Helou Avenue ☎ 01-583 180

Youth and Culture Center

Located in the flowery municipality of Zouk Mikaël near Jounieh, this center houses a library, computer lab, auditorium and cine club. Its library of 30,000 books in French and Arabic makes it a gem to the local community.

🏠 Zouk Mikaël, Municipality Palace Street ☎ 09-213 217 🌐 www.mjczoukmikael.com

Ukrainian Cultural Center

The Ukrainian Cultural Center proposes courses in language, craft, fitness, dance, martial arts, music and song. The TRIUMFF Sports Club, annexed to the center, provides a venue for sports and other happenings and coordinates a cross-cultural exchange serving the Ukrainian community and the neighborhood in which it is located.

🏠 Chiyah, Galaxy Complex, Camille Chamoun Boulevard ☎ 01-559 151
📠 03-735 861 🌐 www.ucclebanon.org

PERFORMING ARTS

Music

In Lebanon, music education is ultimately the parents' responsibility. The school curriculum, which focuses seriously on math, science and language, rarely requires children to learn instruments or anything musical other than, frankly, the singing of the national anthem. Some schools offer extracurricular guitar and piano, but if you're keen on providing your child with a musical education beyond do-re-mi, you'll need to go the extra mile and scout out private resources yourself, as we have done below.

> Lebanon is the perfect place to learn instruments popular in Middle Eastern music, such as the *oud*, a pear-shaped string instrument, and the *derbekke*, a hand-held drum.

> National treasure Fairouz is the most famous living singer in the Arab world.

Lebanese National Higher Conservatory of Music

A source of national pride, the *Conservatoire* was founded in 1930 with a mission to provide gifted students with a superior standard of music performance education. Students take instruction within two distinct departments, Occidental and Oriental, in woodwinds, brass, classical guitar, accordion, piano, percussion and strings as well as voice: opera and classical. A highly-competitive entrance exam and a rigorously-structured curriculum with end-of-year musicianship examinations ensure that only the serious need apply.

 Sin el Fil, Hayek Roundabout 01-489 530 www.conservatory-lb.com
 The Lebanese Higher Conservatory of Music

> The Conservatory's National Symphony Orchestra and Oriental Orchestra perform for free throughout the year. Friday evening performances at Saint Joseph Church in Monnot are a must-hear.

Ecole des Arts: Ghassan Yammine

Founded in 1993 as Ecole de Musique by pianist and composer Ghassan Yammine, the organization currently boasts six branches throughout Lebanon. It offers an extensive course list in the departments of music theory and composition as well as in voice (classical, modern and Oriental). Trains DJs and directs master class choirs. Coordinates onsite and at-home instruction in piano, violin, cello, flute, clarinet, trumpet, trombone, saxophone, oboe, accordion, drums and percussion, with diplomas awarded in affiliation with the National Conservatory in Lyon, France.

🏠 Hamra, Sodeco, Jal el Dib, Ghazir and Beit Chabab ☎ 01-202 820
🌐 www.edmgy.com

Drum Lessons Beirut

Interested in making more than noise in the art of percussion? Aspiring drummers get the rudiments down with professional drummer Samer Zaghir. He studied in London and plays with local bands but perhaps his most impressive credentials are that he's worked with Ziad Rahbani and recorded with Fairouz. Samir gives private lessons by appointment in his home studio to students 6 and older.

🏠 Verdun ☎ 03-779 753 @ drumsens@gmail.com Drumsens

> Guess which famous drummer grew up in Beirut and learned to play here? Stewart Copeland, founding member and drummer of the Police, wrote about his childhood in Beirut as the son of a C.I.A. operative and life with Sting among other things in his 2009 book, *Strange Things Happen*.

KinderMusik

A music and movement program in the same spirit as early childhood development programs Gymboree and Music Together, KinderMusik coordinates musical activities for children ages 3 months-7 years with the aim of stimulating social, emotional, musical and physical development. Classes require advance registration and are held at three locations.

🏠 Achrafieh and Mtayleb ☎ 03-241 020 @ roulaka@hotmail.com
 KinderMusik with Roula

Mozart Chahine School of Music

Born in the late 1960s as Lebanon's leading musical instrument and audio accessories retailer, in 2005 it established a proper music school with a comprehensive curriculum stamped, certified and approved by the Lebanese Board of Education. Teaching instruments and theory, the school has departments in classical, modern, Oriental and music technology. There's also a Little Maestros program for children 7 months-6 years. At-home lessons available.

🏠 Jal el Dib and Zouk Mosbeh ☎ 04-414 649 🌐 www.mozartchahine.com

Modern Music School

German franchise run by the Mozart Chahine School of Music and located within the same building. This department coordinates lessons in rock and pop music and connects fans of these genres with like-minded teachers. Group and private lessons in drums, guitar, bass, keyboard and vocals. For 6 years and older.

🏠 Jal el Dib Highway, Mozart Chahine Building ☎ 04-414 649
🌐 www.lb.modernmusicschool.com

Middle East Audio Suite

Instruction in everything to do with electronic music production, from sound engineering to soundtrack. Opened in 2005, it's the first Digidesign Pro-authorized school in the Middle East. Located in MTV Studios' immense Vision Complex, with its 11 floors and eight fully-equipped production studios. There's also the groundbreaking Groovy Training series for children 5-10 who show an early interest in sound engineering and composition.

🏠 Naccache, Studio Vision Building ☎ 04-444 000 🌐 www.m-e-a-s.com

Parsegh Ganatchian Music College

In the heart of Bourj Hammoud you'll find this school named in honor of the famous Armenian composer and musician. Founded in 1983 under the auspices of various Armenian cultural committees, the college operates within the context of the Hamazakayin Art Center. Its program includes instruction in piano, violin, guitar and other instruments. Houses a music library, hosts annual student concerts and participates in music contests, both local and international. Affiliated with the Gomidas State Conservatory in Armenia; enrollment exceeds 200.

🏠 Bourj Hammoud ☎ 01-249 375 🌐 www.hamazkayin.com
📘 College of Music Parsegh Ganatchian

Rock'n Bach Music School

For students of all ages, the program is based on a method that encourages kids to practice the music they like, together, and provides the opportunity for them to perform in regularly-scheduled public concerts. Both the classical and the modern music options require students to pass two exams a year in order to receive certification from Trinity Music College in the UK. Rock'n Bach stands out for organizing three popular events: Rock'n Donation, Battle of the Bands and Rockwood music camp.

🏠 Ghazir, Joseph Naaman Building, Kfarhbab Highway ☎ 09-850 330
🌐 www.rocknbach.net

La Chanterie de Beyrouth

Popular children's choir directed by Noha Hatem, well-loved music teacher of the Lycée Français. Two generations of francophone children have experienced the joys of weekly rehearsal and vocal training capped by performance in a choral concert before family and friends.

🏠 Achrafieh, Saint Joseph Church, Saint Joseph University Street
📞 03-778 585 or 03-554 618

Janmarie Hagger

Lebanese-American performing arts vocal teacher Janmarie has taken over the reins of the *a cappella* group Beirut Vocal Point and is currently auditioning for a new, as-yet-unnamed group for women or teenage girls. Call for try-outs.

🏠 Hamra   ☎ 03-477 999

> *A capella* is an all-vocal group performance of any style of music. *A cappella* translates from the Italian, meaning "in the manner of the church." In the Islamic tradition, the equivalent style of music is called *nasheed* or *tawasheeh*.

Dance

One great show can inspire a child for a lifetime. The performing arts, however, need a stage. Though Beirut lacks a public performance hall on par with New York's Lincoln Center or the Paris Opera House (the auditorium of the 1948 UNESCO Palace does not come close), sprinkled throughout the city are small theatres and stages which spark pockets of creativity. There's a micro sub-scene of dance and theatre troupes that, once discovered, provide quality entertainment for audiences or a training ground for kids who dream of becoming the next great tragedian. Or *vedette*. Or *fennain*.

> *Dabke* – literally, "stomping on the ground" – is Lebanon's traditional folk dance. Fun, lively, communal and celebratory, it's an expression of the passion of Lebanon's ancient culture and rural traditions. Look for *dabke* class where Oriental dance is taught.

Art and Movement: Alice Massabki Dance Institute

Alice's methodology is all about the alignment and verticality of the spine, but her ideology is that dance comes from the soul. Her twice-weekly classical ballet program demands technical precision, but there's the option of a once-a-week, less strict program that resembles modern dance in that it doesn't insist on the classical line. Pre-ballet for ages 4-6. There's also jazz, hip-hop, contemporary dance and Pilates.

Jal el Dib, La Plaza Center, Block A, Bsalim Road 04-711 536 03-662 600
www.alicemassabki.com

Amadeus

Located in an underground studio, Amadeus is a dance and music school for all ages. It was established in 1998 by Nayla el Hage Habis, who studied classical music at l'Université Saint-Esprit de Kaslik (USEK), the National Conservatory in Lebanon and in Montreal. The music section gives classes in piano, classical singing and opera. The dance section offers classic ballet, Oriental dance and salon dancing.

Sodeco, Sodeco Square 01-612 204 www.amadeusbeirut.com

Beirut Dance Studio

Beirut Dance Studio is known for its professional, dance studio atmosphere and culture of perfection. Founder and director Nada Kano, who studied in Paris with Yves Casati and interned in Madrid, London and New York returned to Beirut in 2001 to open Espace Danse, which, seven years later became Beirut Dance Studio. Classical dance for kids aged 5 and up; classes run October to June and meet daily for adults. This level of excellence doesn't come easy: practice is three times per week. Every two years a dance production is staged, and they are consistently "wow". Encore!

Nahr el Mot, Victoria Building 01-426 869 03-286 869
www.beirutdancestudio.com

Studio Caracalla

Started by Abdel-Halim Caracalla, founder of the world-famous Lebanese dance troupe Caracalla, the school is now run by his daughter Alissar who is a dancer and choreographer in her own right. (She's also the dance professional on the popular, internationally-franchised reality TV program, Star Academy Arab World.) Classes are a mélange of jazz, hip-hop, contemporary, folklore, yoga, Oriental-style and barre. Lessons take place at the Caracalla theatre stage in Sin el Fil. Special kids' classes, theatre workshops and summer dance camps. Think choreography and dramatic dance – fun, creative and liberating.

Sin el Fil, Ivoire Theatre 01-499 904 Studio Alissar Caracalla

> **Caracalla has established itself as Lebanon's iconic dance troupe, creating an original style of Oriental theatrical dance that graces stages the world over.**

El Sarab Alternative Dance School

Its very name holds the promise of unconventionality; in fact, El Sarab envisions a foundation for the "global dancer, mixing all styles under any circumstances." Excuse me? Should this pitch pique your interest, this may be the school for you. Despite the flexible-sounding description, a sound program grants three levels of government-certified diplomas: dancer, soloist and prima. Put more plainly, courses in contemporary, modern, jazz, belly dance and folkdance, conducted by professionals. From age 3.

Byblos, El Haraf Center 09-547 956 www.alsarab-ads.com
Al Sarab Alternative Dance School

Garzouzi Dance Academy

Male ballet dancers are always a breath of fresh air, especially in Lebanon. Mr. Garzouzi is a *ballerin* who's been teaching classical ballet since the 1970s in his dance studio. He also teaches modern jazz and Oriental as well as aerobics and stretching to students age 4 and up.

Achrafieh, Sassine 01-337 089 Academie Garzouzi

Arthur Murray

The American dance school, which has taught social dancing since 1912, is today an international franchise with 300 schools worldwide. The Lebanese branch specializes in ballroom dancing, salsa for singles and couples, the waltz, fox trot, swing, salsa, hustle, Argentine and tango (Is there a style they don't specialize in?). All sessions are a combination of personalized, private and group lessons capped with a weekly practice party. The school also hosts dance sport competition.

🏠 Zalka, El Plaza 323 Center ☎ 01-888 662 🌐 www.arthurmurraylebanon.com

Khanito Dance Academy

Khanito, the flamboyant founder of this dance academy, has more than 36 years of experience in his field. At the academy he prepares instructors, adjudicators, competitors and show performers. For beginners there's a full range of classics from Latin to the waltz, and, especially for kids, fun classes like hip-hop, the cha-cha-cha and tap. Classes meet once a week.

🏠 Zalka, Le Bron Center ☎ 01-878 584 📱 03-224 150 🌐 www.khanito.com

Maqamat Dance Studio

Maqamat offers quality dance lessons in contemporary, Oriental, ballet, Latin and beginner *taijiquane*, which may sound like a Moroccan dish but is actually a form of martial art. Classes and performances for kids include the *dabke* and drama therapy. More than just a studio, Maqamat provides a platform for contemporary dance culture and initiatives to support the dance-theatre arts.

🏠 Hamra ☎ 01-343 834 🌐 www.maqamat.org

Ecole de Ballet: Marguerite Khoury

Madame Khoury's posture says she's a dedicated perfectionist; her CV shows she has taught generations and her studio evokes the retro elegance of yesteryear. She is a teaching member of the Royal Academy of Dance London which sends representatives to Beirut every two years to administer examinations and award certificates to those students who make the grade.

🏠 Achrafieh, Selim Boutros Street
☎ 01-339 064 📱 03-304 890

Nameless Dance Academy

Like playtime, a weekly dance class for children combines Latin, jazz and hip-hop, all in one. For adults, private and group lessons. Founder Pierre Dib pioneered couples dance in Lebanon: he started the Lebanese federation of the International Dance Organization. It's a feather in his cap that in 1994 this academy determined the requisites for certification for the country's dance professionals, teachers and judges.
Jdeideh, Queen Plaza   01-252 525   www.namelessdance.com

> **By law, a dance studio must meet certain standards in order to qualify as an academy. However, as is too often the case in Lebanon, not all businesses abide by the regulations. One easy way to know who is on the up-and-up is to eyeball the premises: if it's smaller than the requisite 400 square meters, the "academy" may fall short of expectations in more ways than one.**

Theatre

Zico House

A lovely, French-mandate town house with rooftop terrace is the intimate setting for this unique cultural center's artistic programs: exhibitions, poetry readings, installations, storytelling, debates, video screenings, dance performances, theatre, concerts, cine club, workshops and more. This special place transforms to meet and nurture the needs of each artist and spectacle that passes through its doors.
Sanayeh, 174 Spears Street   01-746 769   www.zicohouse.org

Zoukak

A theatre company and cultural association that holds classes for kids 6-12 years old in the development of voice, acting, body expression, rhythm and music with fun exercises that focus on creative expression.
Furn el Chebbak Street   70-156 970   info@zoukak.org

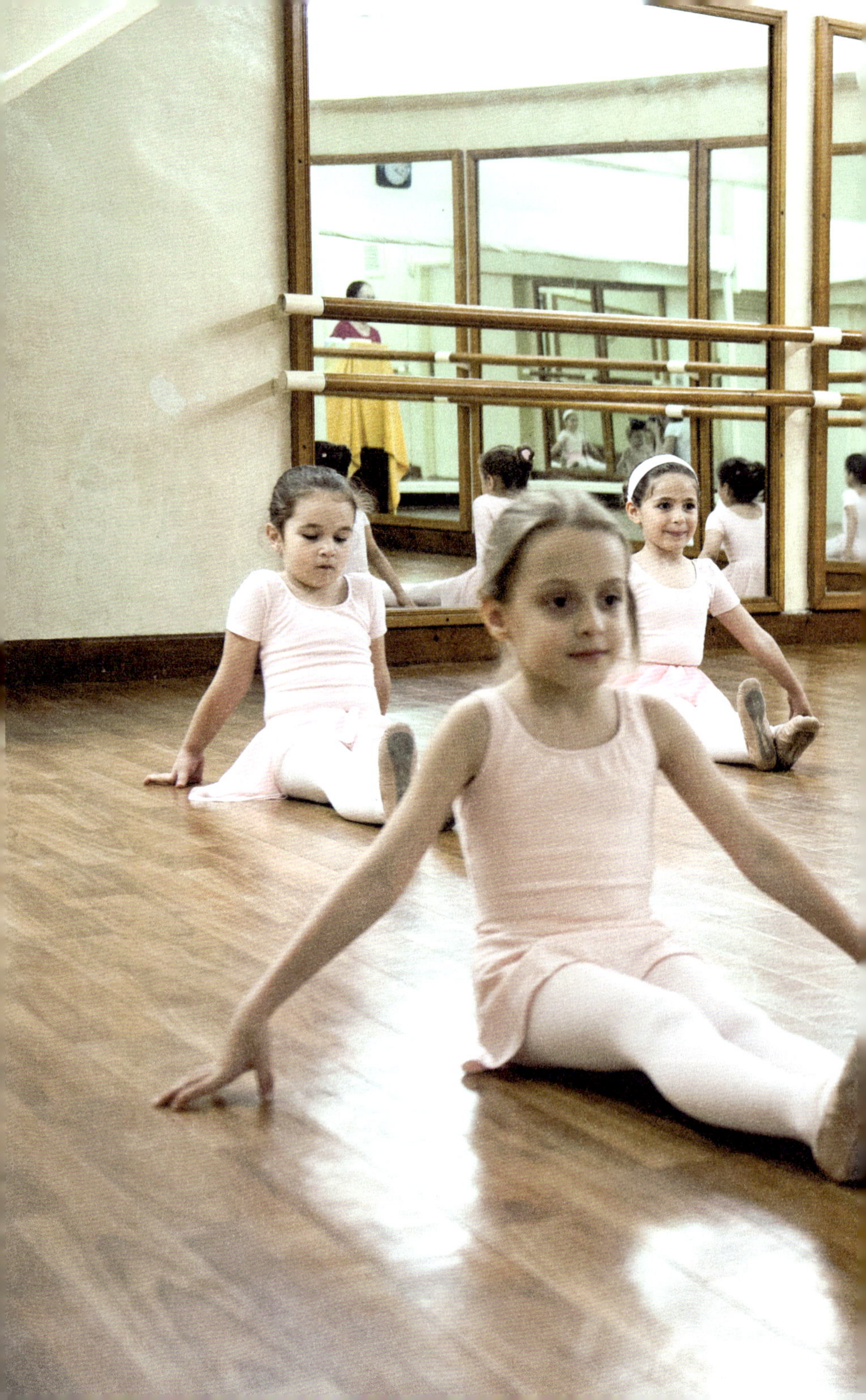

Ballet class at Marguerite Khou[...] Ecole de Ballet

Lebanese Puppet Theatre

Specializing in puppet production and design, the Puppet Theatre was founded by Karim Dakroub with the aim of spreading the art of puppetry in Lebanon. Hosts specialists from abroad to participate in puppet-making workshops. Every November, Dakroub also runs the Caravan Festival – a traveling puppet theatre (see Culture Vulture Calendar).

 Beirut, Tayouneh 01-391 290 www.khayal.org

The Sunflower Theatre

Home to the Lebanese Puppet Theatre, the Sunflower also stages as many as three shows a month, including classical plays, concerts and cultural exhibits as well as plays for children.

 Beirut, Tayouneh 01-381 290 Sunflower Theatre

Ivoire Theatre

AKA Theatre Caracalla, this privately-owned theatre is the sometimes venue for international film screenings but mostly it's known as the home base for the Studio Caracalla dance school.

 Sin el Fil, Ivoire Center 01-499 904

El Madina Theatre

The Al Madina is a vintage, 450-seat theatre – think Beirut in its heyday – that's also the springboard for an arts and culture association founded by the actress/stage artist, Nidal Al Ashkar. (She has played a pivotal role in promoting the theatre arts in Lebanon and the Arab world.) In its role as an arts and culture association, the El Madina promotes a multidisciplinary platform that brings together artists, writers and intellectuals to present their work. Children's theatre productions are also staged here.

 Hamra, Saroulla Building, Hamra Street 01-753 011
 www.almadina-theatre.com

Monnot Theatre

Located on the urban campus of Saint Joseph University (USJ) in an underground building, the Monnot has two stages, the larger with a seating capacity of 285 and the smaller with 80. Among the most active of the country's theatres, it stages 60 productions a year, from local and international plays to readings, dance performances, music concerts and even a film festival.

 Achrafieh, Saint Joseph Street 01-202 422

Atelier Thespis

Atelier Thespis is a theatre association offering instruction in acting, mime and corporal expression for children and adults. Aiming to provide young actors with a solid theatre arts formation in a relaxed atmosphere, the program is divided into three parts: actor's game, mime, and corporal expression. These parts are organized into either non-verbal communication or scenic movement. Classes explore self-expression, feeling and words. Geared primarily toward children 8-12 years old, there's also a special program for those aged 5-6 and another for French Baccalaureate candidates who have chosen theatre as a track.

 Adlieh, Building 63 01-615 594 03-420 945 www.latelierthespis.com

> Atelier Thespis is named for the first actor in history, Thespis of ancient Greece.

Atelier Très-Tôt-Théâtre

If your kids are French-educated and serious about theatre, Michele Malek's troupe will give them a superb formation in the theatre arts. As a teacher at the Lycée Français, she has a reputation for being *exigente* (demanding), a great quality in a mentor. In class, yoga preps body language and vocal exercises hone pitch and tone for perfecting delivery. Look forward to a great performance at the end of the workshop.

 Achrafieh, Victor Hugo Street 03-364 221 Atelier Très-Tôt-Théâtre

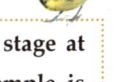

> No listing of stages would be complete without a mention of the stage at Baalbek. Though primarily an archaeological site, the Bacchus Temple is transformed into a spectacular stage set for theatre, music, dance and light shows every summer during the Baalbek International Festival.

Cine Clubs

If your family happens to be into film, there are a number of interesting cine clubs in town, mostly in the French language, but you can find English and Arabic if you know where to look (and we are going to tell you). More good news: admission to these book club-style discussion groups is either free or dirt cheap, making movie night affordable family entertainment, even if you count the pop corn.

Metropolis Art Cinema

Commonly called Sofil, this movie theatre in Achrafieh hosts the Magic Lantern Cine Club for children 8-12 years old. Currently runs nine months out of the year (join so they can continue by popular demand – this club is amazing!). Organized in a fully-realized, didactic way to help children discuss and appreciate films. A week prior to screening, subscribers receive an illustrated journal introducing the film in Arabic, English and French. At screenings, animators present a show related to the movie in all three languages. Such classics as *The Wizard of Oz* take on a lasting, even more magical meaning when presented to children this way.

☎ 01-204 080 (theatre) ☎ 01-332 661 (cine club)

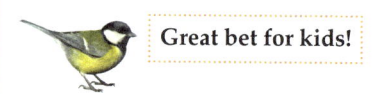

> **Great bet for kids!**

De Prague

Hamra café/pub/resto that shows silent films every evening around 9pm. Most are subtitled in English, some in Arabic or French (call beforehand to find out). Obviously not for the little ones but mature teenagers will totally get the artsy vibe here.

☎ 03-575 282

L' Ecole Supérieure des Affaires

On ESA's Clemenceau campus you'll find one of the best-organized cine clubs in Beirut. Films are always shown in the Fattal Auditorium and are usually screened in French or at least with French subtitles. Some months revolve around a theme. Past themes include Spanish cinema, the new German cinema and "Inescapable Italy."

☎ 01-373 373

Institut d'Etudes Scéniques, Audiovisuelles et Cinématographiques

Carrying the flame for Arabic culture, the IESAV hosts one of Saint Joseph University's two weekly cine clubs. Inside SJU's Theatre Beryte, near Beirut's National Museum, this club screens well-chosen classic and contemporary films in Arabic with French or English subtitles. The organizers make things come alive with the occasional film premiere or guest speaker.

☎ 01-421 000

The Art Lounge

Across from Karantina, where the Beirut River runs dry, this artsy venue directs a popular cine club that's original in that it screens primarily film adaptations of Manga, the Japanese comic book series. Also shows relatively unknown films in French, Arabic or English. Films always relate to an interesting theme.

📱 03-997 676

ART EXHIBITION CENTERS

A great way to capture the zeitgeist of today's Middle East is through the art market. The local art scene is vibrant and sometimes surprisingly experimental. Artistic or not, all children can appreciate, enjoy and benefit from exposure to the art scene, the earlier the better. Encourage younger ones to tote sketch pads to a casual afternoon viewing; bring older ones along to an elegant opening to sip champagne and mingle with artists, collectors and dealers. Here's a list of favorite galleries, few but noteworthy.

Beirut Art Center

In a tricky-to-find neighborhood near Nahr el Mot lies an industrial area with a super alter-ego: the Center of the Universe! – of Beirut's art world, at least. An unassuming former factory removes its Clark Kent-glasses to become (cue: It's a bird; it's a plane...) the Beirut Art Center. BAC to insiders, this well-kept secret has a bohemian vibe that feels like New York's Chelsea and Meatpacking District. The non-profit's founding mission is to "mount solo and group shows of emerging Lebanese artists to complement the permanent exhibitions at government supported museums." So though technically not a museum, at the moment it's the city's unofficial museum of modern art. Besides hosting a number of interesting exhibits and installations, the totally-renovated, loft-like space includes a small auditorium where workshops, performances and concerts run parallel to the art shows. There's also a good art bookshop and a café on the premises, which is off Corniche el Nahr.

🏠 Jisr el Wati, Building 13, Street 97   ☎ 01-397 018   📱 70-262 112
🌐 www.beirutartcenter.org

> Ask at the reception desk for the trilingual Educational Worksheet. Both didactic and dynamic, it provides children with an overview and helps them work through the key ideas and themes presented in the exhibition. Tip: if you're bringing a group of kids, opt for a guided tour. BAC's educational outreach program is supported by the Ford Foundation.

Beirut Exhibition Center

Currently the cultural center of Beirut's new waterfront, the BEC is not exactly a contemporary art museum (see Museums and Arts); it's more a huge art space, managed by Solidère for the purpose of providing the public with free access to an impeccably-curated display of local and international contemporary art. Don't miss a single exhibit. It's interesting to note that the current structure was constructed from the disassembled components of the Children's Museum's Planet Discovery. Now that's amazing in itself.

Beirut Waterfront 01-962 000 ext 2883 www.beirutexhibitioncenter.com

Ayyam Gallery Beirut Tower, Zeitouné Street 01-374 450

Mark Hachem Gallery Minet el Hosn, Beirut Down Town
01-999 313 www.marchachemgallery.com

Sfeir-Semler Karantina, Tannous Building 01-566 550
www.sfeir-semler.com

Aida Cherfan Downtown Beirut, 62 Hussein el Ahdab Street
01-983 111 www.aidacherfan.com

Agial Hamra, 63 Abdel Aziz Street 01-345 213 www.agialart.com

Janine Rubeiz Raouché, Majdalani Building, 1 Charles de Gaulle Avenue
01-868 290 www.galeriejaninerubeiz.com

The Gallerist Sodeco Square 70-545 458 www.thegalleristbeirut.com

---

Just minutes outside Beirut, the Dadour family has constructed the spacious Surface Libre. Surrounded by a manicured garden, the gallery is a place where rambunctious children have the breathing room to view paintings, sculptures and installations, their way. Make sure they bring sketchbooks.

Jal el Dib, Dadour Garden, 77th St 04-716 600 www.surfacelibre.com

CULTURE VULTURE CALENDAR

February

Al Bustan Festival Since 1994, this classical music and performing arts festival has culturally enlivened Lebanon during the winter season. Hosted by the Al Bustan Hotel in Beit Mery, a beautiful, suburban mountain town in the caza of Metn, in the hotel's auditorium as well as at interesting historical churches and other sites throughout Lebanon. With more than 30 performances over a five-week period in February and March, the festival presents mostly chamber music but also opera, orchestra concerts, choral concerts, dance performances, marionettes and theatre, all around a theme (in 2012, Music from Latin America). A complementary visual art exhibition adds effect. ☎ 04-972 980/1/2 🌐 www.albustan festival.com

March

International Festival of Storytelling and Monodrama Organized in 2000 by Saint Joseph University (USJ) in coordination with La Maison des Cultures du Monde in France and the French Cultural Mission in Lebanon, this festival hosts international and local story tellers who delight through the rich heritage of oral tradition. Special daytime performances presented for kids at schools and cultural centers throughout the country; evening performances for adults. Held at Theatre Monnot around the second week of March, from Tuesday to Sunday.
☎ 01-202 422 @ monnot@USJ.edu.lb

Shams Festival Arabic for Spring Festival, Beirut's bi-yearly art festival is hosted by Dawar-al-Shams Cultural Center. The focus is on Middle Eastern contemporary film and the performing arts of music, mime and dance. 🌐 www.dawarshams.org

Little me Little you International Children's Festival Premiering in 2012 under the patronage of the Ministry of Culture and Tourism, this series of events envelopes everything related to stage and theatre production, including children's opera and youth orchestra. ☎ 70-111 096 @ info@scenezgroup.com
f Little me Little you International Children's Festival

April

Little me Little you International Children's Festival (continues . . .) Events and workshops begin in March and run through the end of April. Email for schedule of events. @ limlufestival@hotmail.com

Beirut International Platform of Dance (BIPOD) Since 2004 this festival has been organized by the Maqamat Dance Theatre with the aim of encouraging contemporary dance in Lebanon. Held at various theatre venues throughout Beirut, it also invites international and local contemporary dance companies to participate in workshops, performances and conferences. Every second year, regional choreographers take the stage to showcase dance trends within the Arab world.
☎ 01-343 834 🌐 www.maqamat.org f Maqamat Dance Theatre

AUB Folk Dance Festival: Folkloric dancers from the seven continents grace the stages of universities and other educational institutions during this colorful outdoor spectacle. Coordinated by the American University of Beirut (AUB). ☎ 01-350 000

Garden Show and Spring Festival Now into its ninth year, this exhibit is held at the Beirut Hippodrome and features flower display and competition, nature tourism, garden tips and design as well as handicraft workshops. There are book signings and a kid's village to keep the little ones busy while you shop.
☎ 01-480 081 🌐 www.the-gardenshow.com

Daraj El Fahan Art Festival On Gemmayze's charming Saint Nicholas Stairs, amateur artists display and sell their work. A stroll up or down the steps evokes the artistic feel of Saint-Michel Paris. Encourage your own budding artist to set up shop.
☎ 01-334 267

Fête de la Musique AKA World Music Day, this is an outdoor celebration featuring local artists as well as big international names – you never know who. Organized by the French Cultural Mission, it's an effort to introduce music in all its forms to young artists. This is one night when Beirut's central squares and corners are jamming with concerts. ☎ 01-420 230

Deir el Kamar Festival Meaning festival of the monastery of the moon, this festival highlights the heritage of this magical Shouf mountain town. The architecturally-preserved main square, a historic site that was once an ancient caravanserai, or resting place for caravans, is a dramatic backdrop for this cultural dance and music festival that promotes emerging Lebanese talents.
☎ 05-505 623   🌐 www.deirelqamarfestival.org

Baalbek Festival Lebanon's oldest (since 1955) and most prestigious festival presents world-class performances set amongst world-renowned Roman ruins. This unique festival has evolved into a major cultural event celebrating ballet, theater and all kinds of music: classical, opera, jazz, modern, rock and Arabic and consistently attracts big names, from Sting to Fairouz. For those in the know, attending a concert at Baalbek is on the list of things to do before you die. Starts in July and runs through August.   ☎ 01-373 150/1/2   🌐 www.baalbeck.org.lb

Beiteddine Art Festival In the heart of the Shouf mountains, the courtyard of the Beiteddine Palace, bathed in light, is the evocative backdrop for an eclectic mix of performances in music, dance and theatre. Throughout the years the festival has seen memorable performances by such treasures as Andrea Bocelli, Cirque de Soleil, the cast of Cats, Stomp, Gabriel Yared and Fairouz, just to name a few. One of Lebanon's leading festivals, it dates to 1985, and despite a few pauses during the 2006 War, it has been attracting world famous stars. During festival months, July and August, art is exhibited in the palace's stone arcades.
☎ 01-373 430   🌐 www.beiteddine.org
📘 Beiteddine Festival

Beirut Art Fair A trade exhibit featuring contemporary artists from the Middle East and North Africa (MENA) region. World experts give workshops and lead panel discussions with art world professionals to exchange ideas about the region's evolving art market. An art activity corner is set up to engage and teach children.
 www.menasart-fair.com

Batroun Festival A relative newcomer to Lebanon's festival agenda, this features programs that are divided into two categories: Main Stage (concerts and theatrical performances) and Festivities (fashion shows, movies and children's activities). Attracting international performances such as the musical theater adaptation of The Little Mermaid and British singer Ali Cambell of UB40 fame, the festival adds to the summertime charm of this northern coastal city with its vibrant nightlife.
 06-642 262   www.batrounfestival.org

Tyre and South Festival Started in 1996 and is set in the ancient Phoenician city of Tyre, a city that figures in the history of Alexander the Great and the Myth of Europa. Celebrating Arabic music and culture, performances run throughout July.
 01-791 252   www.tyrefestival.com

Zouk Mikaël International Festival A flowering municipality, Zouk is perched in the hills above Kaslik. Performances are staged in the city's Roman-styled amphitheatre. Attracts a solid selection of international and local artists. Plácido Domingo has performed here, accompanied by the Lebanese Philharmonic Orchestra.
 www.zoukmikaelfestival.org

Byblos International Festival Perched on one of the world's oldest fishing ports, this famous festival features Mediterranean-style jazz, pop and classical music. Though the spectacle of this ancient harbor surrounded by ruins hardly needs embellishment, the festival runs throughout the month.
 09-542 020   www.byblosfestival.org

August

Ehdeniyat International Festival Hosted by the northern town of Ehden, with its not-to-be-outdone attitude, this festival features musical concerts and supports the Lebanese cinema arts. Near the Biblical Cedars of Lebanon.
☎ 01-209 309 📱 03-840 440 🌐 www.ehdeniyat.org 📘 Ehdeniyat

Faqra Summer Festival For one week in August, the posh Faqra Club, a private ski and summer mountain resort, opens its doors to the public, hosting a craft exhibition with entertainment. On sale are smartly-styled decorative accessories and such, backed by dance performances and a famous fireworks display on August 14th, the eve of the Feast of the Virgin Mary. ☎ 09-390 100

Mzaar Summer Festival is a fun-packed, week-long fair in the world-class ski resort of Kfardebian, in the gardens across from Mzaar Intercontinental Hotel. Zones are demarcated by stands: art, boutique and kids. There are shows, music and singing as well as the Xtreme zone with bungee and rocket jumping and skate park.
☎ 09-340 100 📱 03-888 068

September

Liban Jazz As summer winds down, even the music chills. Lebanon's first jazz festival is held at varying venues around town. 🌐 www.libanjazz.com

Beirut Jazz Festival Starts at the end of the month and continues into October. The Beirut Souks is a cool location. ☎ 01-989 040 🌐 www.beirutsouks.com.lb

October

French Book Fair Known to Francophones as *Lire en Francais*, this annual event at the Beirut International Exhibition and Leisure Center (BIEL) is the largest French book fair in the region. Meet well-known authors, attend book launches and find out what's new in the book world. Great educational activities for kids.
☎ 01-420 200/230

Greek Film Festival For the past four years the Lebanese Ministry of Culture, in collaboration with the Greek Embassy in Lebanon, has been hosting this screening at the Metropolis Cinema in Achrafieh. Won't be Greek to you. It's the mirror image of the New York festival of the same name, showing the same films.
☎ 01-332 661 🌐 www.beirutgreekfilmfestival.org

October

Kennel Club Dog Show A contest with an international jury to select the best dog in each breed category. Pooches on parade; we'll say no more.
 www.thekennelclubofLebanon.com

Beirut International Film Festival showcases 20-25 of the year's most interesting alternative feature films, often personal, intellectual and artistic, representing the best offerings from around the world. Always included are a section on culinary and children's films from the international community. Hosts a Middle Eastern film competition and gives awards for best feature film, short film and documentary.
☎ 01-202 411   www.beirutfilmfoundation.org

Vinifest brings the taste of the wine trail to Beirut. Hosted on the lawn of Beirut's racetrack, the Hippodrome, this festival of Lebanese wines features wine tasting, of course, but also musical entertainment and games: trivia contests and activities related to viniculture. At this festival a Guinness world record was set for the largest wine glass (2.4m high x 1.65m wide), which participating producers filled with wine from over 100 bottles. ☎ 01-280 085   www.vinifestlebanon.com

November

European Film Festival Organized by cultural delegations from the European Union, this screening presents a wide range of artsy and original European films. Who knew that sitting in the Achrafieh Empire Sofil Cinema would be one way to plug into the latest film culture in Europe?

Caravan Festival Originally the Mediterranean Puppet Festival, the Caravan troupe tours from March through November, staging puppet theatre and other forms of children's theatre in schools and cultural centers around the country.
☎ 01-391 290   info@khayal.org

Latin American Film Festival A treat for Spanish speakers and fans of the culture, this festival is held at the Empire Sofil in coordination with Latin American embassies in Lebanon and is an opportunity to mix and mingle with the Peruvian, Mexican and Ecuadorian communities.   ☎ 01-204 080

December

Arabic Book Fair features booksellers and publishers from the MENA region that deal in Arabic-language books. There are book launches, author conferences, workshops, readings for children and more. A good starting point to encourage reading in Arabic with a built-in opportunity to buy Christmas gifts as there are often sales promotions. ☎ 01-345 948

Afkart The Lebanese Designers Christmas Exhibition Since 2002, with over 150 exhibitor stands. Organized by the Beirut Association for social development and directed by Nayla Bassili, it supports local talent in the creation of unique jewelry design and home accessories, inspires stylists and much more. Usually takes place prior to Christmas week at BIEL. ☎ 01-566 707 www.afkart.org

Carols by Candle light All Saints Church is a bastion of tradition in the Beirut Central District, with its Sunday services of readings and carols modeled after Kings College, Cambridge. Mulled wine and minced pies are served between services. Always the second Sunday in December. www.allsaintsbeirut.com

AUB Choir and Choral Society Christmas Concerts Annual holiday performance of a classical Christmas choir repertoire, at the beautiful and historically significant Assembly Hall. After the concert there's carol singing and the AUB tree lighting ceremony. ☎ 01-350 000 ext 4350

LAU Christmas Choral Concert Annual Christmas concert performed by the Lebanese American University Choir in the campus auditorium and at the National Evangelical Church. ☎ 01-786 456 www.lau.edu.lb

---

January is hibernation month in Lebanon. Time to take to the ski slopes!

"Lebanon is a museum without walls." **Anonymous**

Museums & More

Cultural patrimony, history, an appreciation of art... these are riches we pass down to our children. For a long time, Lebanon had only two repositories for its public treasures: the National Museum and the AUB Archeological Museum, both in Beirut, both antiquarian. In the past 20 years, however, museums have multiplied in number, expanded in subject and modernized. Today, interesting collections dot the country, exhibiting everything from archeological treasures to soap, from jewels to farm tools and from Khalil Gibran's works to those of the Armenian master painters. Don't forget the Phoenician's purple murex dye! There are quirky, would-be castles and real ones. Children can learn how Neanderthals scavenged Lebanese lands, where three millennia of conquerors left their mark and why Lebanon figures into the fabled Silk Route. The country abounds with unique collections on fascinating subjects that make for charming excursions and fun-filled days.

Museums are free on International Museum Day, May 18th.

BEIRUT

Aristocratic mansions! Ottoman opulence! Sparkling jewels!

National Museum

Lebanon's patrimony, history and heritage are well-preserved and packaged in the country's main archaeological museum. Its collection totals 100,000 objects, of which 1300 artifacts are exhibited. They represent time periods from the prehistoric and Hellenistic, Roman, Byzantine and Arab conquest to the Mamluk (1291-1516). The edifice itself is a clean line, French-inspired, Egyptian revival building of Lebanese ochre limestone specially commissioned to house the nation's treasures. Children who climb its stairs can anticipate the enchantment of discovering booty dug from excavation sites throughout the country, from the amazingly sculpted marble sarcophagi to the majestic Byzantine mosaic of the Phoenician princess Europa, jewelry, coins, pottery, glass, woodwork and more. Kids are especially keen on the two main sarcophagi with enthralling two-dimensional battle scenes. Don't miss the 10-minute documentary about the museum shown in the audio-visual room or the fine old jewels in the upper mezzanine. The museum boutique purveys beautiful gifts handmade by local artisans and interesting books.

🏠 Mat-haf, Museum Square ☎ 01-612 260 🌐 www.beirutnationalmuseum.com
🕒 Tues-Sun 9am-5pm. Closed Monday

Lebanese Prehistory Museum

Cavemen are a surefire hit with children. This small but well-organized museum introduces them to the Paleolithic (1 million-22,000 BC) and the Neolithic periods (6,000-5,000 BC). Tucked away underground on the Saint Joseph University (USJ) campus near the Orient Institute, this museum displays over 500 prehistoric artifacts collected since the late 19th century by Jesuit scholars. Open since 2000, the museum highlights three major themes in the prehistory of the Near East: the advent of tools, hunting and the invention of agriculture. Recreated scenes tell the story of how prehistoric man lived on Lebanese territory. A documentary is shown at the end of the tour. In this setting, a 300,000 Homo habilis skull won't spook the little ones – it demonstrates evolution. No bones to pick there!

🏠 Achrafieh, Saint Joseph University Street ☎ 01-339 702 🌐 www.usj.edu.lb
🕒 Tues, Wed, Fri & Sat 9am-3pm. Closed public and school holidays

Sursock Museum

Lebanon's first modern art museum is located in a 19th century mansion, the historical home of two of Beirut's prominent Greek Orthodox families: the Sursocks and the Bustros. In 1961, Nicholas Sursock bequeathed his villa to the city. Ever since, it has been at the epicenter of Beirut's cultural scene. Famous for hosting the long-running, annual fall art exhibition Salon d'Automne, the Sursock also hosts hundreds of events throughout the year featuring international artists as well as local ones. Its collection boasts more than 5,000 pieces, including paintings, ceramic glassware and iconography dating from the 18th century. The permanent collection includes work from greats such as Chafic Abboud, George Cyr and Elie Kanaan. This exceptional mansion, with its grand, white marble staircase and Ottoman, Italianate and Venetian architectural influences is currently in the process of adding underground floors and parking. Slated to reopen in 2013.

🏠 Achrafieh, Sursock Street ☎ 01-201 892, 01-334 133
🕒 Hours will be posted upon reopening.

Robert Mouawad Private Museum

Aristocrat Henri Pharaon's splendid 1911 mansion-turned-museum by jewelry magnate Robert Mouawad is a showcase for both families' considerable treasures. Located in the heart of downtown near the Grand Serail, the palace resembles a "gothic castle with a hodgepodge of Greek and Roman Statues and sarcophaguses in the walled garden" according to the New York Times. Inside, Pharaon's Dutch Delft tiles, 15th century Damascene ceilings and antique carpets coexist brilliantly with Mouawad's antiquities, icons, Islamic pottery, Chinese porcelain, books, and, of course, jewelry – from the master craftsman's exquisite private collection, which features prominently on the first floor. Like a scene out of a movie about a museum heist, a hidden room conceals a huge diamond revolving in a glass showcase. Other items of exquisite craftsmanship include a 2000-year old funerary stele from Hierapolis, priceless manuscripts, antique furniture and . . . the world's most expensive bra. Super cool.

> Check with the museum for scheduling of seasonal cultural classes.

ℹ️ Henri Pharaon was a Lebanese political personality and nationalist who helped Lebanon gain independence from the French. Bank founder, tennis champion and businessman, he owned the world's largest stable of Arabian horses during the 1950-60s. A great art collector and the richest man in Lebanon for much of his lifetime, Pharaon was mysteriously murdered at the age of 92 in the Beirut Carlton Hotel.

🏠 Zokak el Blatt, Army Road ☎ 01-980 970 🌐 www.rmpm.info
🕒 Tues-Sat 9am-5pm. Closed Monday

Planet Discovery: Children's Science Museum

If you can get past the hidden entrance, or, rather, if you don't pass it up, you'll find a colorful splash of painted steps leading to fun. The only permanent children's science museum in Lebanon, Planet Discovery is designed for children 3-15 years of age but its learning experiences – interactive experiments, exhibitions, performances, workshops and awareness competitions – work for all ages. When it first was opened in 1999 by Solidère in collaboration with the Villette and Palais de la Découverte museums in Paris, Planet Discovery was the only public museum/cultural space in the newly constructed downtown. For this reason it occupies a special place in the hearts of families who raised their kids in Beirut during that period. Now located in the heart of Beirut's Souks, Planet Discovery remains a beloved institution and continues its traditions of puppet shows and birthday parties.

> **The Beirut Souks is a new, bazaar-style marketplace built upon the grounds of the historical downtown souks. Down the lane from Planet Discovery, an ongoing archeological excavation can be viewed through glass.**

Beirut Souks, Ayass Street   01-980 650 ext. 3440
Mon-Fri 8:30am-6pm, Sat & Sun 10:30am-7pm

Underground archeological excavation nestled into the Souks

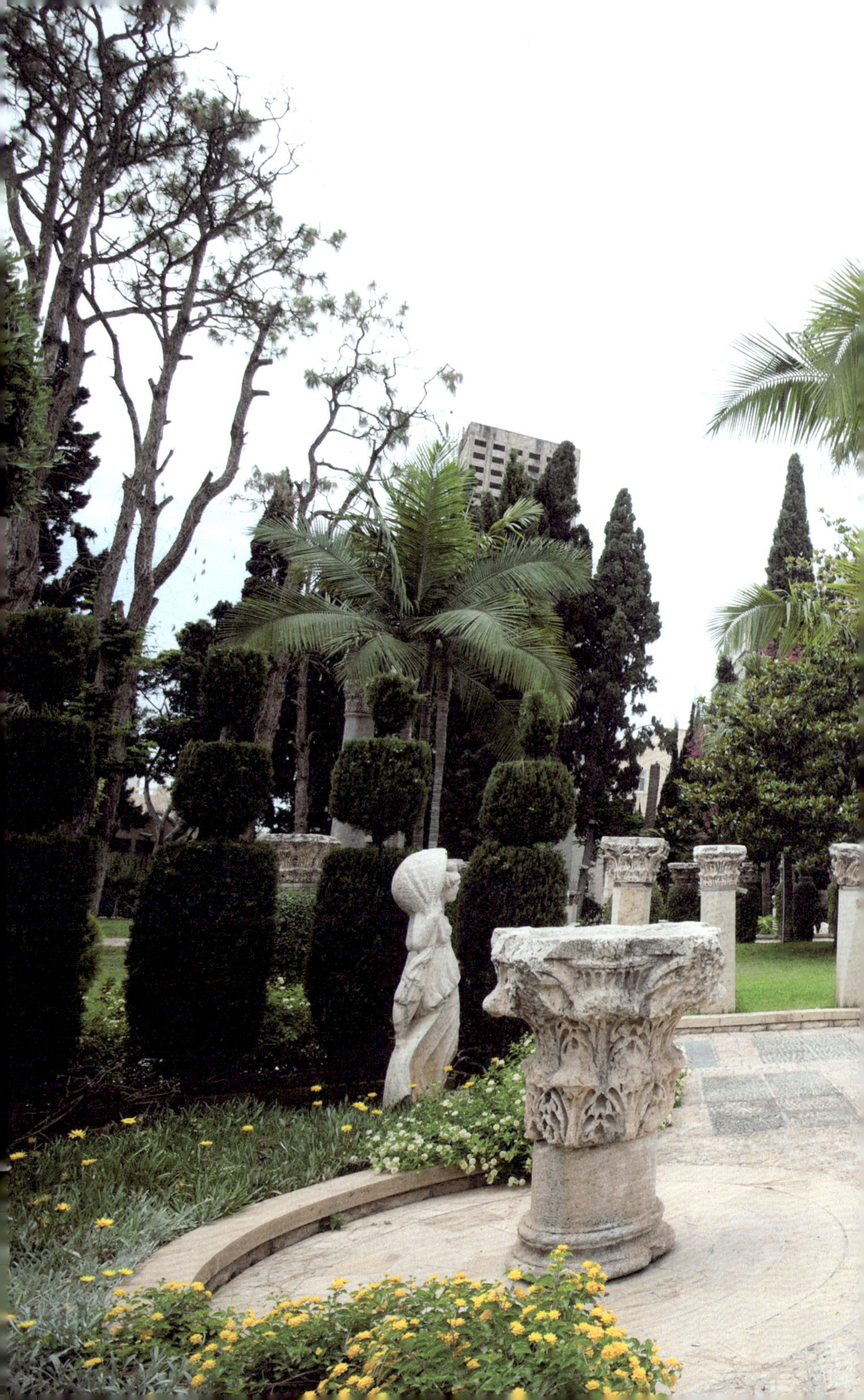

Mouawad Museum's grounds

History and Heritage

Sursock Palace is perhaps Beirut's most well-preserved heritage home. Built in 1860 by Moussa Sursock, the palace and its architecture embody Levantine opulence, an aristocratic lineage to Constantinople, the Ottoman Empire and European nobility. Perched on a hill overlooking the harbor, the palace has been the private residence of the Sursock family for generations. The gorgeous gardens are open to the public once a year as part of Portes Ouvertes, a French Embassy cultural mission that aims to highlight the patrimony of host countries by making their historic homes accessible to the public. The rest of the year, tourists jostle for a snapshot through the main gate; over the years, some have been invited in for a private tour of the grounds by the proprietor, a true gentleman.

Elegant entrance oozing with charm

Details to die for

The romantic Sursock Palace grounds are a super elegant venue for celebrations and are available for hire. The Sursock family also rents out their summer mountain place in Sofar, a paritally restored, circa 1908 fairytale-like palace that when lit up at night looks like a beautiful architectural vestige.

AUB Archeological Museum

Founded in 1863, it's the region's third oldest museum. Nestled on the verdant campus of the American University of Beirut (AUB), the museum in recent years has been renovated and refitted to provide a state-of-the-art experience rather than the dusty-old-stones show of decades past. Here children can relive the transcription of the first letters of the alphabet that made the Phoenicians famous. Although small, the museum is big on education via a wide range of artifacts from Lebanon and neighboring countries which trace humanity's progress from the early Stone Age to the Islamic period. Collections include Bronze Age to Roman period pottery from Cyprus and 10,000 coins dating from the first appearance of coinage (5th century BC). Especially cozy is the Palmyrenean alcove which contains busts from the 1st-3rd century BC. Entrance and exit is through the tempting museum boutique with its fine selection of children's books. If, however, you'd rather not carry, save your purchases for after the visit. Bring a valid ID to enter through the university's main gate; otherwise opt for the entrance near the medical school under the mature, leafy tree.

> The children's program of the Society of Friends at the AUB Archeological Museum hosts art workshops and excursions related to historic and archeological themes. Thumbs up! The society also hosts lectures and trips for adults that are worthy of the membership fee as well as of financial support.

AUB main campus, Bliss Street   01-340 460   Mon-Fri 9am-5pm. Free

MOUNT LEBANON

The Silk Route! World's oldest port! Armenian history and heritage!

The Silk Museum

In the hills just above Beirut, among olive groves and fragrant gardens lie the secrets of silk. Inside the old Fayad family silk spinning factory, purchased in ruins and lovingly restored by George and Alexandra Asseily, live the memories of Lebanon's days as a stop along the ancient silk trading road. Part ecotourism, part history, the museum is concerned with the production of silk from start to finish, including the interaction between humans, insects and plants that brought so many rewards to Lebanon hundreds of years ago. Guided visits through the gardens highlight the region's flora, and there are garden workshops for children 5-12 years old. A permanent weaving demonstration, a new exhibit every opening season and real silk worms! Thumbs up for this charming experience, remembered fondly by so many Lebanese schoolchildren.

🏠 Bsous ☎ 01-744 222, 05-940 767 🕐 May-Sept: Tues-Sun 10am-6pm

> The Silk Museum's sister organization, the Association of Memory and Development (aMed), aims to protect and enhance Lebanon's natural heritage by restoring native flora and fauna, preserving historical buildings and supporting the Lebanese handicrafts culture.

Wonders of the Sea Museum

Impeccable marine museum located in a 19th century Lebanese home and garden. Kids come up close to sponges, crustaceans, corals, starfish, sea urchins and the like. Start with a video-projection about the onsite aquarium, then tour the collections: marine equipment, invertebrates, fish, corals and seashells, the latter being the most important. A 10-minute drive from downtown, just east of Beirut, it's good to get out of town and explore this gem of a museum in its refreshing oasis of greenery with ducks and freshwater fishpond.

📍 Jdeidet el Metn, Assad Yazbeck Residence ☎ 01-891 548
🌐 www.wondersofsea.net
🕒 Oct-June: Mon-Fri 8:30am-1:30pm, Sat & Sun 3pm-5pm.
Jul-Aug: Mon-Fri 8:30am-1:30pm

> **Fun activity:** Next time you collect seashells to paint, don't forget to reference the Wonders of the Sea seashell collection to reinforce the important things your family learned there.

Wax Museum

In the quaint quarter of Byblos, along a cobble stone street, you'll find the Wax Museum, located in a beautiful old stone building just across from the Saint Jean church and a skip from the old port. Using wax figures, the museum recreates scenes from Lebanon's history, creepy to some but popular with kids. Scenes include Phoenician ships, pottery and glass, ancient mythological legends from Adonis, Astarte and Cadmus and important events from the rule of the Emirs to Lebanon's independence.

Wax replica of Khalil Gibran

📍 Byblos, Morcos Street ☎ 09-540 463 🕒 Daily 9am-6pm

Cilicia Museum

The Armenian community is an integral part of Lebanon's rich tapestry of peoples and is close to the heart. This museum pays a moving tribute to their story. It opened its doors to the public in 1998 to display religious treasures brought to Lebanon after the 1915 expulsion of Armenians from their homeland, the ancient region of Cilicia, Anatolia, in present day Turkey. A visit here brings you face-to-face with the community's experience of exodus and the spiritual heritage, treasures and stories that surround it. Located just off the busy highway at Antelias, behind wrought iron gates is a peaceful monastery courtyard with palm trees and jasmine bushes that harks back to a plaza in Yerevan. Go across the courtyard, past the church and bear left to enter the museum at the far end to discover some of the greatest treasures of the world's first Christian state. A guided tour by museum staff brings the displays vividly to life. The collection spans many centuries over three floors: the first floor is reserved for religious artifacts such as ancient chalices, dramatic embroideries, liturgical vestments and triptychs to stone crosses. The second floor, which houses a library for the monks as well as the public, displays a collection of ancient manuscripts, books, bibles and coins. Across the hall, archeological relics as old as the Urartian Kingdom itself are displayed among carpets and tapestries. On the third floor, works from the Catholicosate's collection of modern art by important Armenian painters and sculptors such as Paul Guiragossian and Wartan Mahokian are alone worth the visit.

Antelias, Armenian Patriarchy   04-410 001
www.armenianorthodoxchurch.org   Tues-Sat 10am-5pm, Sunday 10am-1pm

> **In a small courtyard chapel on the grounds, a moving memorial with actual physical remains of some of the victims raises goose bumps.**

> **The museum collection contains the first Armenian Holy Bible and relics dating to the 6th century BC Kingdom of Urartu.**

Hall of Fame

Kitschy and fun for kids, the Hall of Fame displays 50 silicone statues of some of the world's most famous people within the realms of politics, art and culture. Many of the statues sing, talk and move, making for a spoofy outing that gets you giggling.

🏠 Zouk Mosbeh, Jeita Road ☎ 09-225 202/303 🕒 Daily 9am-7pm. Open holidays

Byblos Fossil Museum

Fantastic fish fossils! Features a wide variety of fossils found in the area of Byblos and other regions across Lebanon. Rare specimens from private collections in addition to the museum's collection will pique kids' curiosity, giving the natural sciences some real dimension. The museum has moved just behind the souk and is now adjacent to the archeological site. Open during renovations which are expected to finish by 2012.

🏠 Byblos ☎ 09-540 001 🕒 Summer, daily 8:30am-7pm, Winter, until 4:30pm

Byblos Site Museum

The citadel, or castle as kids call it, is Byblos' main archeological site. An onsite, one-hall museum offers an overview of the excavations undertaken. Illustrating the history of Byblos from prehistory to the Middle Ages, the museum nicely displays finds related to these periods as well as thematic panels detailing the daily life of ancient inhabitants.

🏠 Byblos Citadel ☎ 09-540 001 🕒 Summer: Daily 8:30am-7pm, Winter: Until 4:30pm

Expo Hakel

Hakel's fish don't spoil, even after 100 million years. That's because they are extracted from mountains and forever fossilized. Open since 1991, this is the first museum in Lebanon specializing in local fossils. Above Byblos, in his native village of Hakel, passionate collector Rizkallah Nohra restored an old house in which to display his collection of over 500 specimens, which include rays, sharks, eels, worms, crustaceans, crinoids and plants. It's worth noting that the majority of these species are now extinct.

🏠 Byblos, Hakel Main Road ☎ 09-770 012 📱 03-708 287 🕒 Daily 8am-6pm

Louis Cardahi Foundation and Museum

Located in a stone house with a red-tiled roof, just south of Saint Jean-Marc Cathedral, this cultural and museographic center focuses on the long, rich history of Byblos. The first-floor exhibition room juxtaposes ancient artifacts with modern urban paintings and contains a library of books and documents. The refurbished basement displays old photos as an audiovisual projection narrates the ancient port's history in Arabic, English and French.

 Byblos, Mina Avenue 09-540 310 www.louiscardahi.com
 Sat 9am-4pm, other days by appointment.

Pepe Abed Museum

In the days when Lebanon was the Paris of the Middle East, Pepe Abed's fishing club restaurant on the picturesque port of Byblos was a favorite stop for the jet-set. What most don't know is that adjacent to the restaurant, he set up a museum in an 800-year-old residence to display his personal collection of antiquities. UNESCO currently supervises the museum.

 Byblos, Old Port at Fishing Club 09-540 213 Mon-Fri 10am-4pm

CHOUF

Lives of the Emirs! The Cedars of Lebanon!

The Shouf Cedar Museum (hope springs eternal)

Gotta love Lebanon. The Shouf Cedar Museum is listed left and right on the internet and even in Ministry of Tourism brochures, but if you call the number given, they'll tell you wearily that there is no such thing. It's not a museum; it's only an "environmental awareness center" for the country's largest natural forest reserve, featuring specimens of biological diversity: plants, butterflies and reptiles. Is it too much to expect a museum at the site of Lebanon's proudest symbol? Hello?! We're talking about the Biblical Cedars of God, here. We think Lebanon's cedars merit a museum, so we're holding this place.

 Shouf, Ain Zhelta, Environmental Awareness Center 05-350 150/250
 www.shoufcedar.org Daily 9:30am-4pm

Beiteddine Palace Museum

A real emir's palace, built between 1788-1818 by the Emir Bashir Shihab II. Beiteddine's architecture and garden grounds tell the story of grandeur connected with Lebanon's Ottoman Empire. No family should miss roaming among the inner court yards resplendent with fountains, Turkish baths with a glimmering glass dome and opulent *liwans* (Arabic salons) overlooking breathtaking valley views. The ground floor's stone arches serve as a nice exhibit space. The museum displays ceramics, glass, sarcophagi, jewelry and a significant collection of Byzantine mosaics.

> **Beiteddine Palace, site of the annual Beiteddine Festival, is the sometime summer residence of Lebanon's presidents.**

Beiteddine, Caza Shouf 05-500 077
Apr-Oct: Tues-Sun 9am-6pm, Nov-Mar: 9am-4pm. Closed Monday

Marie Baz Museum

Located inside the walls of the old palace of Emir Fakhreddine el Maani II, this museum relates the history of Lebanon since 1512 through a collection of 100 wax statues of well-known personalities, from Lebanese presidents and poets to foreign dignitaries, all of whom have left their mark on history.

> **Upon entering you'll see a short version of yourself in a mirror that distorts and dwarfs, a reference to the legend that Fakhreddine was so short that when an egg fell from his pocket, it wouldn't break!**

Deir el Qamar, Shouf 05-511 666   03-756 000
Summer: Daily 9am-8pm, Winter: Until 6pm

Moussa Castle

On the road to Beitedinne, you can't miss this ostensibly medieval castle. A curiosity at best, but kids really like it. Usually there's a camel stationed across the street giving rides for a fee. Hand-built, stone-by-stone, by the eccentric Moussa Maamari (1945-2006), this fanciful museum was his lifelong dream. A panache of wax models depict scenes from the daily lives of nobles and peasants. There is also a sizeable collection of rare weapons. After the tour, bitter Arabic coffee is served in an old-style setting, adding a taste of authenticity.

🏠 Beiteddine, Shouf ☎ 05-500 106 📱 03-273 750 🌐 www.moussacastle.com.lb
🕐 Summer: Daily 8am-8pm, Winter: Until 6pm

BEKAA

Roman ruins! Rural traditions!

The Traditional Lebanese House Museum

Here you'll find a varied collection that includes old weapons, Roman capitals and columns, Lebanese currencies, photos of Lebanese presidents, rare Persian carpets, colored glassware, furniture and musical instruments.

🏠 Zahleh, Barbara quarter ☎ 08-822 170 🕐 By appointment only

Terbol Eco-Ethnographic Museum

A project of the National Heritage foundation in the historic Bekka Valley, an indigenous adobe-mud brick farmhouse – the last one standing – has been restored and transformed into a museum to record the rural and agricultural history of the house itself and the region. A video documents how a rural woman named Fudda retains her knowledge and skills about repairing, painting and decorating the interior walls of an adobe house. How charming to discover the farmer's way of life through the minute details of every niche in this dwelling. You'll also appreciate learning about the environmental sustainability of this building method.

🏠 Terbol, Saint Talka Church ☎ 05-455 104 📱 03-987 67
🕐 May-Nov: Daily 10am-6pm

Baalbek Site Museum

Baalbek's history and excavations are related through a series of panels documenting rich archaeological finds including statues, mosaics, sarcophagi, ceramics and more. Inaugurated in 1998 to commemorate the 100th anniversary of Emperor Wilhelm II's visit to Baalbek (now there's a story for the kids – not only about the largest Roman ruins in the Levant but also about the Germans' love of archeology). Make sure to check out the old pictures taken by German photographer Herman Burckhardt.

🏠 Baalbek Citadel ☎ 08-370 520 🕒 Summer: Daily 8:30am-7pm, Winter: Until 4:30pm

Ras Baalbek Eco Museum/The Traditional Molasses Press

Opened in 2009, the Traditional Molasses Press is the second eco museum to open under the patronage of the National Heritage Foundation. Ensconced within a 200-year-old workshop with original vat, well, millstone, hearth and cauldron, visitors learn about the age-old method for producing *dibs* (carob molasses) *à la façon* Ras Baalbek, the type specific to the region. Follow the arrows, peruse old documents, view the photos and tools and watch the audio-visual projection that brings the elderly villagers' oral histories to life.

🏠 Ras Baalbek ☎ 05-455 104, 01-367 753 🕒 May to Nov: Daily 10am-6pm

> In the museum's garden, there is a typical *tannour* oven used for baking bread since ancient times.

SOUTH

Soapmaking! Sea life! Ottoman architecture! Famous Phoenicians!

Soap Museum

Soap and Saida go together. Generations ago, the Audi family manufactured saboun baladi in their factory near the souk. Transformed into a museum and open to the public since 2000, it's a loving, in-depth tribute to the history of soap in Lebanon and the region. Authentic vats under vaulted stone arches and traditional Lebanese architecture impeccably restored and outfitted with the latest museology make a visit here a major treat. Immaculate displays of the tools and accessories used in soap production and ancient bathing rituals include such interesting objects as ornate Turkish *hammam* bath shoes and an eclectic array of soap molds. Demonstrations of how to make the traditional soap used by generations of Lebanese families out of bay leaves, olive oil and essence of rosebuds feel relevant again considering the return of all things natural. The soap museum is a tried-and-true thumbs up activity for families.

 Saida, El Moutran Street, Haret Audi 07-733 353 or 753 599
 www.fondationaudi.org Mon-Thurs, Sat & Sun 9am-6pm. Closed Friday

> Bring home a bag of inexpensive saboun baladi for kids to carve with plastic knives and mold with clay tools into whatever they like.

History Museum of Saida

The 18th century Debbane Palace is a showcase for decorative architectural motifs styled after the Damascene school, originating in Mamluk traditions and embellished with Ottoman opulence. The Debbane Foundation has been working to restore the building to its former splendor by transforming it into a museum that illustrates the impact of the Ottoman Period on Saida's rich architectural history.

Saida, Moutran Street
07-720 110   www.museumsaida.org
Mon-Thurs, Sat & Sun 9am-6pm. Closed Friday

The Phoenician Museum

Lebanon's patrimony is tied to the tides of the Levantine coast. This museum relates the history of ancient Tyre and the legend of the Phoenician's maritime prowess. Don't miss the big hall's collections from the sea.

Tyre, Chawaqir   07-740 874   03-803 376   Daily 9am-5pm

Lebanese Museum for Marine and Wildlife

Exhibits marine creatures collected from Lebanese shores, displaying more than 2,000 species. Just so you know, among them are no less than 35 species of Mediterranean sharks alone. Get up close to the giant basking shark (9m, 5 tons) and a giant dolphin (3.5m & 400kilos). They're in there!

Jeita   07-343 017 or 09-222 054   03-246 317   Daily 8am-7pm

NORTH

Gibran Khalil Gibran! World sculpture! Medieval printing press!

Gibran Khalil Gibran Museum

Gibran was, of course, a writer, poet, philosopher and artist, but in Becharreh, he will always be the favorite son. The author of *The Prophet* chose for his final resting place a mountain crevice snuggled into the Monastery of Mar Sarkis (Saint Sergio) in the town of his birth. In 1975, this hermitage overlooking the Valley of the Saints was made into a museum. The contents of Gibran's New York studio, including his furniture, personal belongings, manuscripts and 440 original paintings (190 of which are exhibited) are on display in the museum. A truly touching hometown tribute befitting an artistic genius.

🏠 Becharreh ☎ 06-671 137 🕐 Summer: Daily 10am-6pm, Winter: Daily 9am-5pm

Basbous Family Art and Sculpture Exhibition

The Basbous name is synonymous with modern sculpture. In 1994, the three Basbous brothers, sculptors all, hosted an international sculptural symposium in their native village of Rachana. It ran for 11 years. Four years later, on 2,500 square meters of family ground, Alfred Basbous opened the International Park Museum, displaying more than 75 works from 66 sculptors from around the world. The family intends to resume the annual symposiums, which were interrupted due to political circumstances. In the meantime, at the alfresco museum and in two indoor museums, families can observe not only works honed from marble, wood, iron, bronze, aluminum and stone, but how close Lebanese families work together.

🏠 Rachana, Batroun ☎ 06-720 903 @ zeinabasbous@hotmail.com
🕐 indoor museums by appointment; outdoor museum open always

Saint Anthony the Great Monastery Museum

The museum in the monastery is a worthwhile stop on a trip to the Qadisha Valley, a UNESCO World Heritage site. Here is the first printing press in the Middle East (1585), religious artifacts and gifts from kings mixed in with a bric-a-brack of clay pots and agricultural tools.

🏠 Zgharta, Arbet Qozahaya ☎ 06-995 505
🕐 Summer: Daily 9am-8pm, Winter until 5pm

Debs' designs capture zeitgeist

Think you'd always recognize the Middle Eastern aesthetic for classics such as the backgammon board and mother-of-pearl inlaid mirror? They have been brilliantly reinterpreted by Lebanon's iconic designer Nada Debs, who has a knack for creating cult classics.

Her work has become famous internationally because it epitomizes the essence of the modern Middle East. Debs' customized art installations have been featured in museums from Europe to the Far East.

Luckily her creations also grace our own galleries, stores and restaurants. See how her traditional furniture and objects breathe fresh air and stand in contemporary elegance at her boutique in Zaitunay Bay and showrooms in Saifi Village.

Debs' "Gran Papa" backgammon board made of walnut, inlayed with mother-of-pearl and tin

"If you have a garden & library, you have everything you need." **Marcus Cicero**

Public Gardens & Libraries

Every great city has its peaceful green spaces and great libraries, right? New York has Central Park and the New York Public Library; London has Hyde Park and the London Public Library, and Beirut has. . . OK, Mr. Cicero, maybe Beirut does not have *everything*. Not yet, anyway. Post-war Beirut is still getting its footing in terms of urban planning and does not have gardens or libraries on par with the international standard. Maybe soon, Solidère's planned Normandy Park on the waterfront will become the place to bring a book. Until then, we have only a handful of neighborhood parks and three municipal libraries around the city, all the more valuable because of their rarity. Before we throw the book at Beirut, however, or think its parks 'shady' in the pejorative sense, consider that twenty years ago, there were no municipal libraries at all and public parks were few, frail and faded. Lebanon is making progress.

Can you believe there's free Wi-Fi during working hours in 11 public parks (mostly in Beirut)?

PUBLIC GARDENS

"A garden is a friend you can visit anytime." – **Anonymous**

Gibran Khalil Gibran Garden

An oval shaped public square in downtown Beirut, located smack dap in front of the landmark ESCWA (United Nations Economic and Social Commission for Western Asia) building. A bust of the Lebanese American poet, author and philosopher is set amongst two circular lawns, a fountain and some modern sculpture. The space lies at the intersection of two busy streets but is protected on both sides by immense walls of concrete (intended to protect the UN from terrorist attacks). In the recent past, the garden has been used as a venue for peaceful demonstrations and sit-ins, so check the news before you find yourself mingling with picketers.

Jesuits Garden

Also known as *Yassouhiye*, this peaceful oasis is located in the Remeil district of Beirut, in a neighborhood straddled by two hospitals: the Saint George and Jeitawi. Monkey bars, swings, slides atop a sandy play area. Birds chirp and old people occupy park benches, walking sticks in hand, enjoying the sights and sounds of children playing. Inside garden gates, an adorable public library exudes a garden conservatory feel. Park and library in one gem of public space: Lebanon could use more spots like this.

Sanayeh Gardens

Officially renamed the René Moawad Garden for the president who was assassinated near here in 1989, but everyone still calls it Sanayeh, the name of the neighborhood in which it is located. It's probably the oldest public park in Beirut (1907) and has the magnificent mature trees to prove it. Near busy Hamra, the park gives off an authentic city park atmosphere. It bustles with walkers, joggers, playing children, even artists exhibiting their work; there are the requisite elderly sitting on benches in the shade, playing cards, backgammon and chess. At the main entrance, vendors sell colorful pinwheels and other wares. There's a paved area for rollerblading and a bike track; a bike rental shop is across the street. Note the kids playing ball under the "No Ball Playing" sign. They'd do better to head to Horsh Beirut Public Park for soccer.

Garden of Forgiveness

Hadiqat as Samah in Arabic, this space has long been in development by Solidère in the downtown center where it straddles an archeological site flanked by two churches and two mosques. The garden's name reflects the concept that lasting peace can only be achieved when people are able to embrace forgiveness. The garden is meant to be a place of contemplation and reflection for healing the country's war wounds. World-renowned landscape architect Kathryn Gustafson has been charged with fulfilling this formidable task. How ideal it will be to one day sit in this garden and have a cross–generational and confessional dialogue that is sensitive to Lebanon's thorny history and breeds understanding and compassion.

> **Gustafson also designed the Diana Memorial Fountain in London's Hyde Park and has received many international accolades.**

Horsh Beirut

By far the largest urban park and incidentally the least known. Also called Horsh el Sanawbar or, in French, Bois des pins (both mean pine forest), the park covers about 300,000 square meters of green space within municipal Beirut. Near the Hippodrome, it lies close to the old airport road. At the park's periphery you'll find three free public tennis courts, three basketball courts and five soccer fields, three of which are quarter size, one half size and one full regulation size. Proper city park with free admission and free parking.

> Horsh Beirut's central gardens have been closed to the public for nearly twenty years but the issue of whether to reopen them is currently under public debate.

Saint Nicholas Garden

Public square/garden located on Charles Malek Avenue facing Saint Nicholas Church. In 1964, Lebanese architect Ferdinand Dagher designed a gracious, European-style public garden outfitted with a central rectangular fountain pool (often empty of water), statues and well-manicured hedges. In practice, it's a neighborhood square, dotted with chatty housekeepers keeping watch on playing kids and walking dogs. There's a taxi stand located at the main gate.

Sioufi Garden

Located in the residential area of Sioufi, on the periphery of Achrafieh. This ample, sprawling park is set on a hill overlooking the Beirut River and has a view of Mount Lebanon. Paved walkways cut into the side of the hill wind their way across the expansive landscaped park, creating a romantic feel. There are two playgrounds with swings and slides, a pool and a mini water cascade. Love birds flock here to sneak a kiss on a park bench under a tree. Some mornings a Tai Chi class takes place in open-air.

Roman Baths Garden

Landscaped with terraced patios designed for open-air concerts and plays, this archeological park is located on the steps below the Grand Serail, just above the impeccably restored Roman baths.

Beirut Waterfront Park

The future epicenter of the city. Today it stands as open land, straddling the seaside with terraced waterfront walkways. There's a popular corniche/promenade, perfect for walkers, bikers and rollerbladers. Children test their remote control cars and ride scooters on broad, freshly-tarred roads for pedestrians only. Check it out pronto; take advantage of its raw openness, fresh air, sea views and sunlight before it succumbs to inevitable real-estate development. This view of Beirut's skyline won't last long.

Horsh Beirut public garden and park

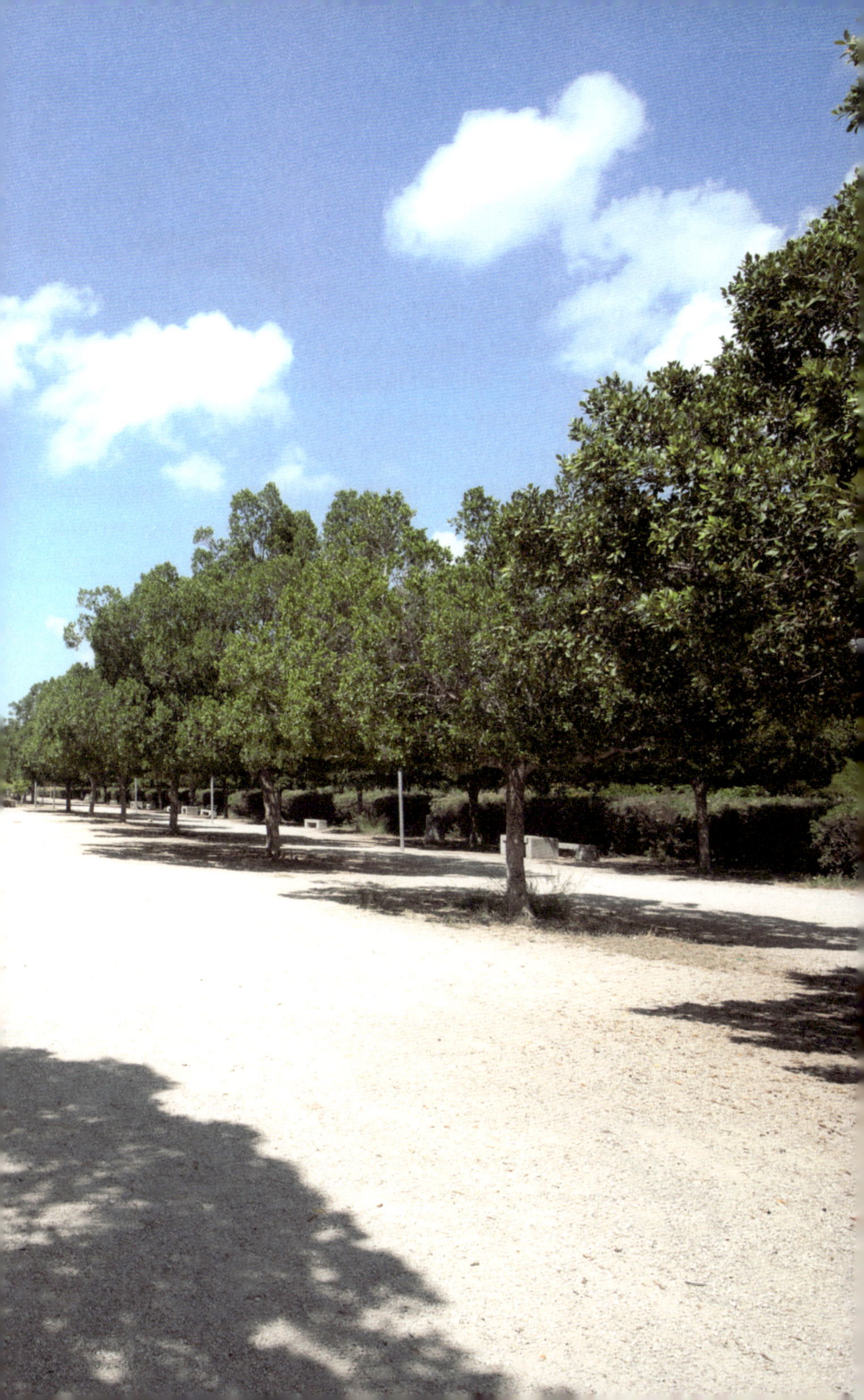

LIBRARIES

"A book is like a garden carried in the pocket."
— Chinese proverb

The Arabic proverb "He who lends a book is an idiot. He who returns the book is a bigger idiot" illustrates the mindset that had to be overcome for public libraries to work. And they are working. At present there are three new city libraries and many more opening across Lebanon. Including the French Institute's revamped lending library, all provide a framework to encourage reading. Free books, story time, poetry readings, writing workshops, meet the author . . . a library card is a passport to the world and a giant leap in quality of life for children being raised here.

> To get a library card you'll need:
> 1. Identity card
> 2. Completed application
> 3. One passport-sized photograph
> 4. A one-time deposit of 10,000LL
> 5. Written permission from parent if under 15 years of age

Note: You can borrow as many as four documents for up to three weeks.

Let's give credit where credit is due: for the new libraries, we have to thank Beirut's municipalities and France, but mostly Assabil (the Friends of Public Libraries Association), the Lebanese non-governmental association (NGO) founded in 1997 to establish and promote public libraries in Lebanon that are free and open to all. Assabil works with the Ministry of Culture to coordinate promotional events throughout the year such as the annual reading week which takes place in mid-April. The NGO also assists in managing libraries, distributing books and organizing training sessions and workshops.

ℹ️ Beirut was designated World Book Capital in 2009. According to the selection committee, which included UNESCO, Beirut was chosen "... in light of its focus on cultural diversity, dialogue and tolerance and because of its diverse and stimulating program." This was much-needed recognition and encouragement for Lebanon's efforts to give books their place.

Municipal Public Library of Monnot

Small and quaint, it is just one step down from the sidewalk in a smartly decorated space with stylishly reupholstered 60s reading chairs. Open since 2008, its book collection focuses on film, theatre and the arts, which makes wonderful sense considering its location near Monnot Theatre. Good selection of English books, both fiction and nonfiction, and a cozy reading corner around the magazine and newspaper section.

📍 Achrafieh/Monnot, Saint Joseph Street ☎ 01-203 026 🌐 www.assabil.com
🕒 Tue-Fri 10am-6pm, Sat 10am-1pm

Municipal Public Library of Jeitawi

The second municipal public library to open in Beirut is located in the Jesuit Garden, in the Remeil neighborhood. No bigger than a room, this adorable library has a garden conservatory feel, with ceiling-to-floor windows that bring the outdoors in. Bamboo shades, brightly colored Lebanese tiles and walls lined with well-worn paperbacks are deco details adding to the intimate charm. The garden setting is inspiration for a niche book collection on the environment which currently stocks 50 books on topics ranging from gardening to ecology. The general collection totals 7,000 titles. There's a comfortable children's section with colorful cushions and two community computers free of charge. It feels good here; the place calms your nerves while expanding the mind and is great fun for kids. Note that the library closes for lunch – kids can play in the garden in the meantime.

📍 Jeitawi/Achrafieh, Jesuit Public Garden ☎ 01-562 677 🌐 www.assabil.com
🕒 Tues-Fri 9 am-1pm, 2pm- 6pm, Sat 9am-1pm

Municipal Public Library of Bachoura

Couldn't be more central, across the Ring facing the downtown. Opened in 2000, Beirut's first public library is a 300 square-meter space on the third floor of the Isaaf Building in Bachoura. It has a wide collection that includes newspapers, magazines and games for all ages. It has books in Arabic, French and English and also stocks some materials in Armenian, German, Tamil, Amharic and other languages. The large open space includes a children's area, a newspaper corner, internet access, photocopying, reading tables and some comfortable chairs. The library hosts regular events such as storytelling, puppet shows and guitar concerts. A security guard is posted at the building's entrance because the Beirut Police Department and Civil Defense Department share the space. You can take the elevator up when there's electricity; otherwise come in shape to climb three flights of stairs with your books in hand. If this is a problem, call the library in advance for the electricity schedule.

Bachoura, Isaaf Baladi Building   01-667 701   www.assabil.com
Mon 9am-1pm, Tues-Sat 9am-1pm

> The Bachoura and Jeitawi libraries host a weekly story hour every Friday for their youngest visitors as well as a monthly film club, which is popular, particularly among teenagers. They regularly welcome visits from schoolchildren. For adults there are evening poetry readings, musical performances and discussions.

> If you have old books or free time to donate, the Friends of Public Libraries Association is a bibliophile's best friend.
> Ras el Nabeh, Naoura Building, Mohammad el Hout Street   01-664 647

La Médiathèque de Beyrouth

The most comprehensive French library in Beirut, the Médiathèque is an integral part of the Institut Francais, formerly the French Cultural Center. Opened in 1993 and refurbished in 2008 with a special youth section dubbed "Book Island", its three stories of shelves contain a fully-stocked library and media center of more than 27,000 books, 2,500 CDs, 1,500 DVDs, 150 magazine titles and all the French newspapers. Activities such as weekly story time revolve around the collection. More than a *salut* to French literature, la Médiathèque contains a collection of French books translated into Arabic.

Mat-haf, Damascus Street   01-420 256/7   www.institutfrancais-liban.com

Baakleen National Library

Ensconced in a historic 1897 building, the Baakleen Saray, the one-time court, prison and gendarmerie post. In 1987 the building was restored and furnished with volumes, reference books, periodicals and all the accoutrements needed to assume its new identity as a public library. It's worth a visit just to see the building, never mind the children's library collection of more than 10,000 titles. All year long, but especially during the summer, the library hosts programs for children ages 5-14. Run by a well-trained and experienced staff and holding books in Arabic, English and French, the Baakleen National Library currently boasts the largest public library book collection in Lebanon.

Chouf, Baakleen Saray   05-304 051   www.baakleenlibrary.com

The National Library

An important cultural institution in Lebanon. Established in 1929 by Viscount Philippe de Tarazi, it suffered during the Lebanese Civil War (1975-1990). Its doors closed; its collections were scattered into temporary shelters and its very existence erased from the consciousness of the post-war generation. Currently the library and its collections are undergoing major restorations with the goal of reopening in 2014. It will hopefully soon regain its status as the crown jewel of Lebanon's public libraries.

Viscount Philippe de Tarazi

1921

Viscount Tarazi donates his personal collection to Lebanon and it becomes the core of what he calls "The Great Library of Beirut"

1940

The start of the library's golden age with patronage of intelligentsia from around the country and region

1975

Historic manuscripts

On the eve of the Lebanese Civil War, National Library holdings include more than 200,000 books, documents and manuscripts including important historical and administrative archives left by the Turks in 1918 as well as documents from the French Mandate years

1979

The library's activities are suspended

Meticulous restoration

1991

The Lebanese National Library Foundation is established to make the institution's rehabilitation a national priority

Portraits of Lebanon's intellectuals that once graced the library's reading hall sit in storage awaiting the reopening of the National Library.

PUBLIC LIBRARIES OUTSIDE BEIRUT

Following is a list of Assabil's municipal library network. When in the area, you might want to pop in and check out the libraries' diverse collections and reading facilities or support them by donating some of your own books. Contact Assabil for further information on any library.

Assabil
Ras el Nabeh, Naoura Building, Mohammad el Hout Street 01-664 647

Shouf
- Public Library of Aitat
- Public Library of Baadarane
- Public Library of Barouk
- Public Municipal Library of Hammana
- Public Municipal Library of Joun

South
- Public Municipal Library of Aitit
- Public Library of Babliye
- Public Library of Saida
- Public Municipal Library of Jezzine

North
- Public Library of Batroun
- Public Library of the Cultural League in Tripoli
- Public Library of Kefraya el Koura
- Public Library of Miniara, Akkar

North Metn
- Public Municipal Library of Bocsmaya
- Public Library of Beit Mery

Aley
- Public Municipal Library of Aley

Bekaa
- Public Library of Hermel
- Public Municipal Library of Zahleh

Mtein
- Cultural Center for Francophone Activities

Mount Lebanon
- Public Library of Khreybet Chouf

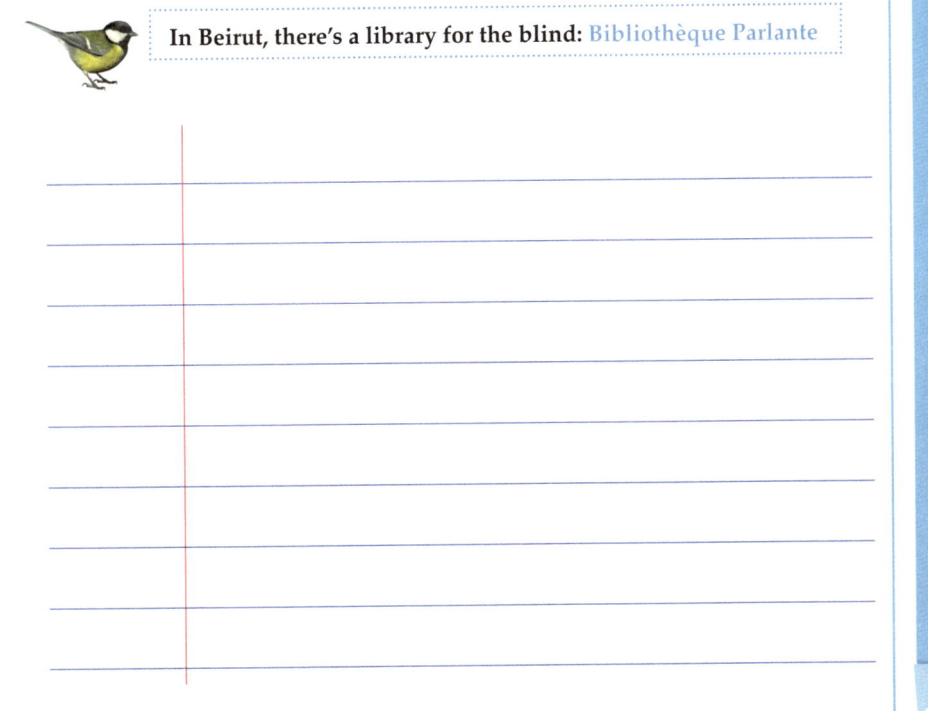

In Beirut, there's a library for the blind: Bibliothèque Parlante

"…the earth delights to feel your bare feet and the winds long to play with your hair." **Khalil Gibran**

Snow Sensation

Skiing in Lebanon is congenial and convenient thanks to snow-capped mountains, a temperate climate and short driving distances. It's a winter paradise if you're well prepared and know how to navigate the mountain resorts as well as the powdery slopes. The season stretches from December to April and major ski stations are an easy drive up for a day trip, weekend or extended vacation. If your family dreads downhill action, just head for the hinterland, which is always open and free for cross-country, snowshoeing, snowmobiling or just having a blast messing around with the snow. However, resorts are best for learning to ski or snowboard. In this chapter we detail the main resorts. Many Lebanese have a favorite, as they tend to do with most things, sweet shops included. Finally, the Lebanese love to brag that in Lebanon you can ski and swim in the same day, a tired old cliché but true. Once you know how to zip from the slopes to the seaside, you're in for an unforgettable sensation that very few places on earth can offer.

Getting prepared

Regarding safety, it's an unfortunate fact that parents everywhere must be vigilante when leaving a child in the care of a stranger. Lebanon is no better and no worse than anywhere else. Whether your child's ski instructor is Swiss-trained or a ski bum from the *daya'a* (village), you must ensure that your child knows in advance what to do should he or she become uncomfortable with an adult.

Safety First

- Wear a helmet – it's required
- Prior to hitting the slopes, warm-up to lengthen and strengthen muscles
- Dress in layers, in quality ski wear that's both water and wind resistant
- Make sure gear accords to weight, height and level of skier
- Protect eyes and skin from the strong ultraviolet rays of the Lebanese sun
- Drink water to guard against dehydration and bring snacks
- Stay on the trail; don't stop in the middle
- Respect distances when passing
- If you fall, move off the trail immediately

Gearing Up

Graduated Length Method (GLM) for choosing proper ski length according to child's skill level:

- Novice: 2" shorter than child's height
- Intermediate: just below child's height
- Advanced: skis at child's height

All the major resorts rent equipment. If children will be skiing throughout the season, long-term rental is more economical than by-the-day.

FARAYA MZAAR

Sometimes referred to as Mzaar, after the Mzaar InterContinental hotel in nearby Ouyoune el Simane, this is the most popular and best equipped ski resort in the country. Its 42 slopes and 80 km of trails are big and busy, good for moderate to advanced skiers looking for a challenge. If you fancy training your children to ski competitively, this is the right place. Recreation from bowling to movies and the Kids' Fun Center will keep your family busy off-slope, too. The resort is also known for its 'see and be seen' scene, complete with nightlife, restaurants, spa and more.

- **Altitude:** *1,913-2,465m*
- **Distance from Beirut:** *46km; 1hr 15min*
- **Directions:** *Take the Autostrade towards Jounieh. At Nahr el Kalb pass through tunnel then move to right lane. Exit at Zouk Mosbeh. Follow main road up.*

Faraya Mzaar Accommodations

Faraya offers options for every taste and budget, from the luxurious and costly Mzaar InterContinental and small boutique hotels to furnished chalets and the family-run auberges.

Mzaar InterContinental Mountain Resort and Spa

Faraya's main hotel and the epicenter of the action. The country's leading ski resort is a village within a village located right at the base of the slope, a five-star deluxe hotel and spa with recreation. The terrace of Le Refuge restaurant is the place to work on your winter tan; it's directly at the foot of the hotel's private slope. The lobby lounge, great for cocktails and mingling, has a fireplace and a Belgian chocolate/tea salon – the perfect spot for an après-ski hot chocolate. Dining options are many, from Lebanese, Italian and Latin American to buffet, fondue and raclette but kids will like the new sports café. Adults can dance until dawn at the onsite nightclub then turn into one of 131 well-appointed rooms. For families, the loft is a roomy, chalet-type option on the hotel's top floor. Indoor recreational facilities include a bowling alley, billiards, squash court, heated pool, fitness center, gaming area and a movie theatre. There's a shopping arcade selling Versace and furs. Les Thermes du Mzaar spa offers packages.
☎ 09-340 100   www.mzaar2000.com

Eleven

Boutique hotel with exactly eleven nicely-appointed rooms, including five suites, each uniquely styled, all with the requisite fireplace. The on-premises restaurant has a cheese cellar with 50 varieties. Cozy and within walking distance to slopes.
☎ 09-341 741   www.hotel-eleven.com

Gio

Upscale mountain chalet-style accommodation equipped with nine cozy rooms. This auberge has spectacular views overlooking both the valley and the Mediterranean Sea. It's simple and clean. Ski equipment is included and can be stored directly in the room. Same owners operate the Montagnou and San Jose furnished apartments just 100m away.
03-489 111   www.montagnou.com

Auberge le Valais

Swiss auberge-style hotel with 12 rooms, one suite, a garden and playground. Two restaurants: one with Swiss cuisine, the other traditional Lebanese. Reasonable rates.
☎ 09-341 227   03-552 227   www.aubergelevalais.com

3S Cottage

Private chalet complex on the plateau of Ouyoune el Simane. Ideal for families, it has common areas, a swimming pool, underground parking and recreation room. Same faces tend to rent year after year, making for a close-knit, family-friendly environment. Recently renovated, the chalets are for sale but also available for direct rental from owners.

☎ 01-201 588 📠 70-400 755 🖥 www.3scottage.com

Merab Hotel

This small, three-star hotel's location right in the village square makes it central and convenient. Near the Mzaar InterContinental, the neighborhood mini-market and the slopes, it's owned and operated by the brothers Bteich, who also own the supermarket and restaurant next door. Reasonable rates.

☎ 09-341 341 🖥 www.merabhotel.net

Merab Deluxe Suite

Sibling of the Merab Hotel just across the street, it offers seven small, self-catering apartments outfitted with kitchenettes, which is, for families, always convenient because it circumvents the cost of dining out three times a day.

☎ 09-314 341/0 🖥 www.merabhotel.net

Chateau d'Eau

Located in the valley below Faraya Village, it's a drive away from the action and slopes. Considering winter road conditions, this may not be your best bet, but keep it in mind if all else is full, which is often the case. Reserve addresses do come in handy when travelling with the family.

☎ 09-341 424 🖥 www.chateaudeauhotel.com

San Antonio

Just above Faraya village, this intimate lodge with 28 rooms, some connecting, resembles a hostel, complete with cheerful lobby and charming fireplace. There's a small recreation room with billiard table and a place to play cards.

☎ 09-341 048

Faraya Mzaar Restaurants

Montagnou

Modeled after a Swiss chalet, this restaurant has bay windows and terraces that overlook spectacular mountain views. Run by a restaurateur well-known in Lebanon, it specializes in fondues, raclettes and pierrades, classic comfort foods for the alpine scene. Meats are succulent and the fondues tasty. Delicious food served in a wonderful atmosphere. Thumbs up! A family favorite in Faraya.

☎ 09-341 441   📱 03-290 678   🌐 www.montagnou.com

Chez Michel

Serves delicious Middle Eastern cuisine in an affable atmosphere; warm, ambient rustic décor. A loyal clientele raves that Michel's grilled kebab is the best in town.

☎ 09-300 615

> **Forewarned is forearmed: table dancing has been known to happen here in the evening.**

Manakish Oum Bashir

Classic Mom and Pop *man'oushe* stand. Oum Bachir uses the traditional *saj* oven and prepares your order right in front of you. Fresh and warm, it's the stuff of memories. Located on the main road at the village entrance. Just ask the locals.

☎ 09-321 117

Faraya Mzaar Ski Schools and Clubs

Mzaar Ski School

Staff of 100 qualified, trilingual instructors takes exceptional care in teaching children and adults to ski. You can find them in the Ouyane el Simane parking lot. Fee includes priority access to ski lifts and insurance.

📱 03-722 217

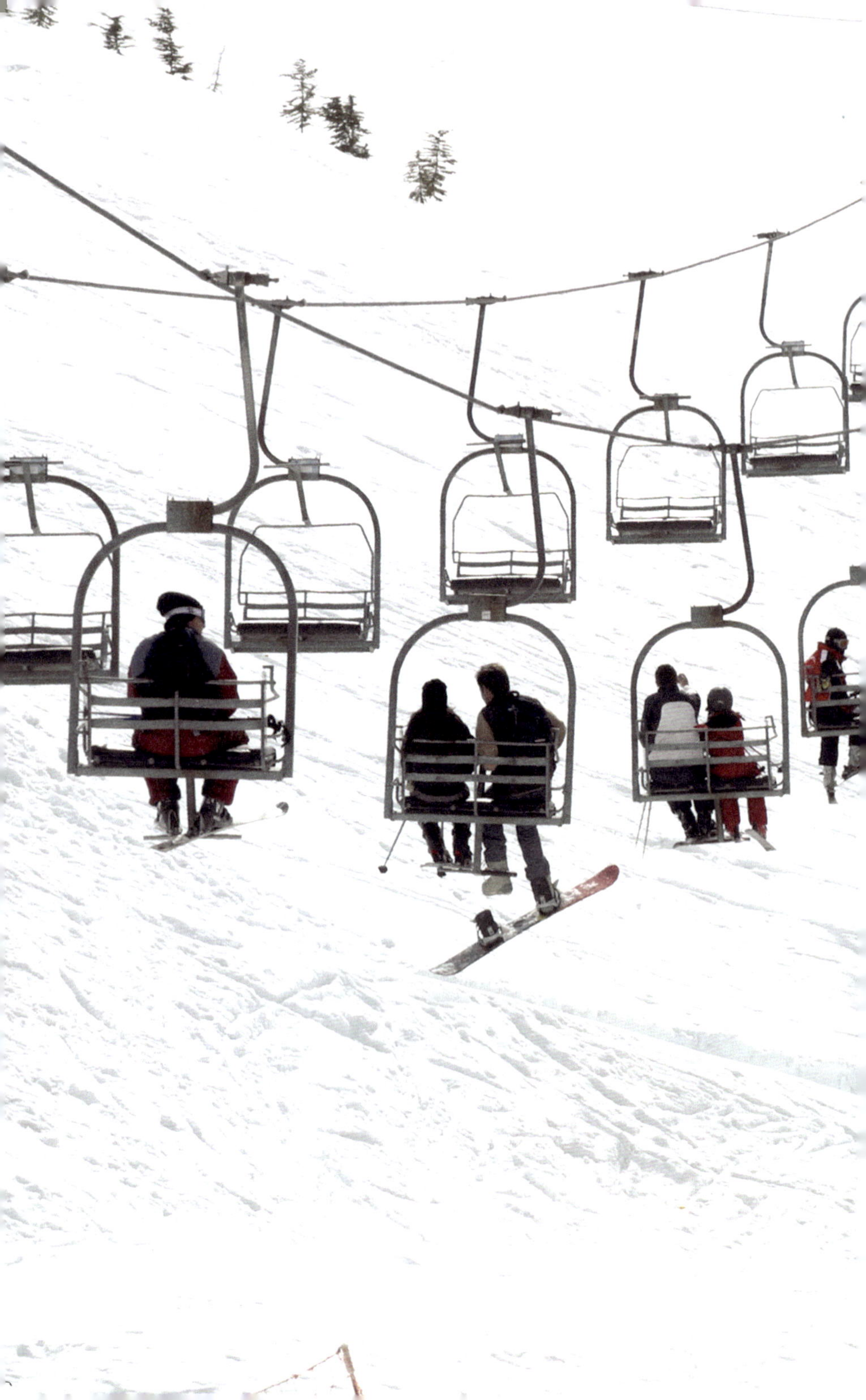

Ski lift at a major resort

Le Club des Sports Faraya

A competitive ski school operating since 2000, offers lessons at two locations: the Ski School at Warde and the Ski Club at the Refuge. The club organizes competitions in all categories and has trained many young champions.

🌐 www.faraya-mazaar.com

Mountain Masters

Ski school operated by the winter division of kid's club Vacances et Loisirs, or V.E.L.

☎ 01-880 962   📱 03-251 710   🌐 www.groupevel.com

Groupe Z

Your kids want to ski for the day, but you're too busy to leave Beirut? Zeid Bteich runs a ski school that can be of great service to parents who cannot accompany their kids to the ski resort. A bus picks them up from a central meeting point in Beirut for a day of skiing. Fee includes breakfast, group lessons with a ski instructor and insurance. A convenient option for children aged 5-14.

📱 03-696 962 or 70-696 962

Enfants du Soleil

Instruction for children and adolescents. Organizes outings and promotes physical and social well-being through winter sport. Kids are encouraged to participate and compete with group spirit.

☎ 01-902 915   📱 03-778 203

Raja Saade

Popular snow boarding school with experienced instructors. Raja's shop, Yellow Cab, in Aljaltoun sells and rents snowboarding equipment.

☎ 09-273 193   📱 03-288 193

> **Children younger than five ski for free at the Faraya Mzaar resort but arrangements should be made ahead of time at the office opposite the Mzaar InterContinental.**

FAQRA

The mountain air is rarified at Faqra, and so is the clientele. Just outside the entrance gates, an ancient temple some believe to have been dedicated to Adonis rises from the rocky landscape. This ski utopia in Kesrouan is a private, gated community with good suburban planning, organized streets, charming villas and green spaces. The Faqra Club is posh: members only and their invited guests have access to the private restaurants, swimming pools, squash and tennis courts plus all the conveniences of well-maintained facilities. Exclusive, yes, but the down side is that due to lower altitudes, Faqra gets less snowfall than Faraya. However, Faqra is more child-friendly, smaller to navigate, less crowded and more accommodating for beginning skiers (there's a designated lift for babies!). The Alpine ski school is staffed by highly qualified Swiss and French-trained instructors. Five private slopes (two certified by the International Federation of Ski) provide world-class, safe facilities. For all these reasons, Faqra is the preferred destination for school ski trips and camps.

☎ Faqra Club 09-300 601   🌐 www.faqraclub.com

- **Altitude:** *1,735-1,975m*
- **Distance from Beirut:** *45km; 50min*
- **Directions:** *Take the Autostrade towards Jounieh. Keep right after the Nahr el Kalb tunnel. Exit at Jeita and drive up the Faraya road past Faytroun, Mairouba and Hrajell. At Faraya roundabout, drive straight through for about 2km then take left turnoff. Pass army check point and Chez Michel hotel. Turn right at Faqra roundabout.*

There's a new game in town: green skiing, a sport that involves sliding on grass. At present, Faqra is the only resort in the Middle East to offer green skiing, and plans to organize competitions. Should be great for kids' spring and summer recreation.

Faqra Accommodations

Auberge de Faqra

Opened in 1981 as a Relais & Châteaux hotel. Although it hasn't kept this association, it has kept its classic elegance, which was further updated with a 2010 renovation. Its lobby is a magnet for interesting guests. Offers rental rates for both the three-month ski season and the summer season.

☎ 09-300 600   www.faqraclub.com

Terre Brune

Located just outside Faqra's gates, this hotel has 40 rooms and some suites, all decorated with earth tones and rich wood furnishings. Floor-to-ceiling windows open onto balconies with mountain views. Stylish lobby complete with fireplace, pool, gym and new spa. Free shuttle service to slopes. A favorite for families looking for *rapport qualité-prix*.

☎ 09-300 060   03-030 301   www.terrebrunehotel.com

LAQLOUQ

The countryside amid Laqlouq's apple orchards is serene and beautiful; just imagine it covered with snow. With its gentle slopes, Laqlouq is one of Lebanon's smaller, cozier ski resorts – it's truly family-friendly. Catering mainly to beginners and intermediate skiers, the Laqlouq Village Vacances resort is equipped with seven lifts: three ski lifts, three chairlifts and one *fil neige*. It seems customized for kids but there's something for everyone, including International Ski Federation-approved slopes for competition, one for giant slalom and another for special slalom. Laqlouq provides a quiet, laid-back environment and is nearly free of buildings and construction in comparison to other ski resorts. Nature, peace and quiet: perfect from a parental point of view, it's an ideal place to introduce young ones to snow sports. Besides the slopes for alpine skiing and sledding, you'll find a flat terrain that's excellent for cross country and snowshoeing. Slopes open at 7:30am and close at 3:30-4:00pm during weekdays and 4pm during weekends and holidays.

- **Altitude:** *1,650-1,920m*
- **Distance from Beirut:** *66km; 1hr 15min*
- **Directions:** *Take the Autostrade towards Jounieh. At Nahr el Kalb pass through tunnel then move to right lane. Take Jbeil exit. After Annaya, turn right at army checkpoint. Follow road to Ihmiji village just below Laqlouq resort.*
- **Nearby places of interest:** *the Afqa Grotto and the caves at Balou*

Laqlouq Accommodations

Shangri-La

Family-style, family-run hotel, managed under the banner of Laqlouq Village Vacances. Accommodations include 20 rooms, some connecting. Reception area is simple yet cozy with a sitting room off to the side which is equipped with board games. There's also a recreation room with a ping-pong table and billiards. The dining hall serves good, home-cooked, family-style meals.

☎ 09-430 006   📱 03-441 112   🌐 www.lakloukresort.com

Nirvana

Annexed to the Shangri-La hotel, Nirvana is a dormitory-like building with 30 rooms. Here you'll find a semi-Olympic-sized pool, which is good, but if you have the choice, the Shangri-La is cozier.

☎ 09-430 006   📱 03-441 112   🌐 www.lakloukresort.com

Private chalets

Simplex, duplex and three-room resort-owned chalets are available to rent either for a few days or for the winter season. This may well be the most charming option at Laqlouq Village Vacances.

📱 03-256 853

QANAT BAKISH

The smallest and least developed of Lebanon's ski resorts, Qanat Bakish has been catering to locals since the 1960s. It offers quality snow in a low-key setting that's great for beginners. It's also good for cross-country skiing. The only hotel, the Snowland, operates two ski lifts and the ski school. Parents can relax in the restaurant while watching their children ski. Slopes are open from 8am-3:30pm weekdays and 8am-4pm weekends.

- **Altitude:** *1,800m*
- **Distance from Beirut:** *47km; 1hr*
- **Directions:** *Take the Autostrade towards Jounieh. At Nahr el Kelb pass through tunnel then move to right lane. Exit at Jeita. Pass Ajaltoun and Faitroun then turn right toward Mrouj. Follow signs for Snowland Hotel.*

Qanat Bakish Accommodations

Snowland Hotel

Family-run hotel with 35 rooms with either sea or mountain views; family and connecting rooms available. Inquire at hotel about organizing a group tour of the Qanat Bakish region.

☎ 04-252 222   📱 03-340 300   🌐 www.snowland.com.lb

> A local claim to fame is that on a clear day at Qanat Bakish, you can see as far as Cyprus.

CEDARS

The Cedars in Becharreh, Lebanon's first and oldest ski resort, is named after Lebanon's national tree, *al arz*. The nearby, ancient cedar forest, now a protected reserve, is the heart and soul of this area. Skis need never touch your feet to appreciate the majestic trees that date to biblical times, but to slalom near these wonders is an incomparable feeling. The Mount Makmel slopes form a magnificent natural amphitheater and the lifts are situated within its huge basin. Enjoy uninterrupted forest views and glimpses of the fabulous valley below. Runs are long with lots of *hors piste* options for more adventurous skiers. There's good snow depth for most of the season. Several snow-wire lifts on gentle slopes serve beginners. Slopes open from 8am-4pm. A paradise for nature lovers and history buffs, the Cedars remains incredibly uncommercial, a miracle that adds immeasurably to the spirituality of the place.

- **Altitude:** *1,850-2,810m*
- **Distance from Beirut:** *around 180km, 3hrs*
- **Directions:** *Take the Autostrade toward Jounieh. Take Chekka exit and go left at the sign for the Cedars. Drive 45mins to Becharreh and go right.*

ℹ At 3,088m, Kornet el Sawda is the highest peak in the Middle East.

Cedars Accommodations

L'Auberge des Cedres
Adorable Swiss chalet-style boutique hotel with cozy, well-appointed rooms and inviting character. Some separate private chalets.
☎ 06-678 888   www.smresorts.net

Saint Bernard

Old world, chalet-style hotel with spacious outdoor terrace and fabulous views. Regular clientele adds to the homey ambience of this family-run hotel with onsite restaurant and nightclub.

☎ 06-678 100   📱 03-289 600   🌐 www.hstbernard.com

St. Peter's Hotel

Facing the Cedar Forest, near the residential chalet quarter, this hotel's advantage is its private slope, perfect for beginners. The convenience of onsite ski instructors and equipment rental, including Ski-Doo and ATV, is a godsend for families, making us wonder whether we've all died and gone to heaven and are at the gate of St. Peter's.

☎ 06-678 055 or 03-321 490   🌐 www.hotelstpeter.com

Auberge Eco Club

Surrounded by vast slopes, this eco friendly rural lodge with tent-style accommodations is natural fun for the whole family. The lodge also serves as a summer camp for kids. During the rest of the year it offers sports and touristic activities like hiking, biking and cross country skiing.

☎ 06-671 595   📱 03-832 060   🌐 www.ecoclub-becharre.org

Mon Refuge

Budget, family-run hotel within walking distance to the Cedar Forest and neighboring hotels. Downside: the busy décor may be an affront to the design-sensitive. Upside: you're likely to bump into the friendly owner who does his best to make you feel at home.

☎ 06-678 050   🌐 www.lebanonchalets.com

Alpine

Fifteen studios and four furnished chalets at reasonable rates that include breakfast buffet and a kitchen that never closes. The indoor recreation room is equipped with baby foot, ping pong and pool table. The outdoor area has a few flowers in a garden patch and open views to the valley. Hotel arranges for paragliding. The owner loves to say, "Alpine is your home in the Cedars." Reservations are made directly through him.

☎ 06-678 099   📱 03-213 102

If you're feeling courageous and want to get your adrenalin pumping, or if you just can't resist the view, try paragliding over the Cedars.

Cedars Restaurants

Hotel Saint Bernard
Family-style hotel restaurant serving Lebanese cuisine as well as pizza, spaghetti and steak. House specialty is the St. Bernard fondue.
☎ 06-678 100 / 101   📱 03-289 600

Le Chaudron des Cèdres
AKA the Alpine Hotel, serves steaks, escalope, pizza, burgers and spaghetti as well as classic Lebanese fare. Fifteen indoor tables plus an outdoor terrace in summer.
☎ 06-678 099   📱 03-213 102

The Lodge (L'Auberge des Cèdres)
Restaurant and nightclub serving salads and soups and Arabic, French and Italian cuisine in an amicable atmosphere. Après-ski favorites such as fondue, charcuterie and cheese are big here.
☎ 06-678 888

ZAAROUR

Zaarour is small but closest to Beirut. Located in the Metn, on the western flank of Mount Sannine and managed by Zaarour Country Club, the ski station has five slopes served by ski lifts and a snack bar. For chalet owners, there's the private, year-round Zaarour Country Club. Nowhere near as posh or elegant as Faqra; still, Zaarour's amenities include squash and tennis courts, a heated swimming pool, gym, nursery and amusement center. Slopes are open to the public, but it's best to call and check for access and availability. Overall, the resort is fairly well-organized and secure, with first-aid and orderly queues to the slopes, which are open from 8am-4pm. Alpine skiing is leisurely here; the general pace suits beginners. If your family is up to a cross country skiing adventure, take the 4km route over the Mount Lebanon range.

☎ 04-310 010

- **Altitude:** *1,850m*
- **Distance from Beirut:** *54km, 1hr*
- **Directions:** *Take Antelias exit off the Autostrade. Continue up Bikfaya Road toward Dhour el Choueir then follow signs. Alternatively, take the new highway from City Mall in Dora and follow signs from there.*

Zaarour overlooks the Valley of the Skulls, so named because for hundreds of years it has been the final destination of countless unfortunates who were unsuccessful in navigating the mountainside's steep and narrow road.

Following are some touring companies that organize winter activities for kids and families.

Dreaming of participating in a snow man competition? **Neo Kids** is a touring company specializing in family tourism. It hosts all kinds of fun winter activities.
📱 03-733 818 🌐 www.neoslb.com

Interested in a Ski-Doo adventure? **Snow Xtreme** organizes winter activities throughout the country from their base at the Mzaar resort.
📱 70-755 756

Snow shoeing, Ski-Dooing and other snow sports, **Promax Adventures Lebanon** will customize an adventure to please your family.
☎ 01-871 443   📱 03-955 642   🌐 www.promaxsports.com

Snowboarding and Ski **Club Thermique** offers daily excursions.
☎ 09-237 193   🌐 www.clubthermique.com.lb

Cross country skiing, connecting with nature and exciting escapades are the specialties of **Blue Carrot Adventure.**
📱 03-553 007   🌐 www.blue-carrotadventure.com

> **La Reserve Afqa is a nature reserve (see Eco Tourism and Summer Camps) that organizes snow survival camps on weekends during January and February.** ☎ 01-498 775/6   📱 03-727 484

> "Never, no never, did nature say one thing and wisdom say another." **Edmund Burke**

Nature

This generation of kids gets to enjoy Lebanon's natural beauty. After years of woeful neglect, the government has committed to preserving the country's biological and ecological significance. Today kids can go wild in any of seven official nature reserves and several protected areas. Or, for a more cultivated outing, tour one of Lebanon's prized vineyards, where families are welcomed like long-lost relatives come home to help with the harvest. Discover open-to-the-public farms, places where crops are grown and animals kept, including a monastery and an old TB sanatorium. Natural beauty hides in every corner of this land, every crevice and contour of its landscape, topography, flora and fauna. In this chapter we reveal Lebanon's hidden beauty and the secrets to enjoying it.

ECO TOURISM EXTRAORDINAIRE

"In every walk in nature one receives far more than he seeks." – John Muir

Eco tourism, visiting natural, usually protected habitats is the new vogue. Reserve some time to visit the country's nature reserves, which number seven thus far. Get out in the woods. Hike Lebanon's mountain trails and tour its rural villages. You'll discover a timeless beauty and an agricultural abundance that'll inspire your family to respect the environment and to celebrate nature's nurturing spirit. Foray into the forest individually, as a family or as part of a group. Every way, it's an opportunity to connect with a national heritage and feel like a bona fide eco warrior.

Reserves

Palm Islands Park and Natural Reserve

Welcome to a fertile breeding ground that's been designated a Mediterranean Specially Protected Area under the 1995 Barcelona Convention. Not to be mistaken for Dubai's Palm Island, Lebanon's Palm Islands are 30 minutes by boat or six nautical miles north-west off the coast of El Mina. Within this natural marine basin lie three separate islands: Sanani, Fanar and the largest, Palm Island, dubbed Araneb (Rabbit) Island because of the exponentially multiplying rabbit population noted at the time of the French mandate (early 20th century). Today, all three islands are part of an important bird and wetland reserve where diving, turtle monitoring and wild life photography are encouraged. Bring your binoculars to the bird watching tower to see 156 species of migratory birds fly over. Enjoy the sandy beaches; they are of global importance as an egg laying site for the rare Loggerhead turtle. Take a dip in the protected waters of this archipelago and be on the look-out for rare sponges and replenishing fish species.

Directions: Take a boat from El Mina, the port district of Tripoli.

www.moe.gov.lb

Open to the public Jul-Sept; off season, access only with special permit for education and research purposes

> **Palm Islands are home to the only sea bird nesting site in Lebanon.**

Tyre Coast Nature Reserve

Just south of Tyre, this 400-hectare reserve claims some of the best-preserved sandy beaches in the country. The reserve is divided into three zones: the tourism zone's sandy beaches are open to the public for swimming. The conservation zone consists of sandy dunes and fresh water ponds; it's an important coastal eco system where marine scientists collect data and conduct research. For this reason, visits are restricted and require permission. The agricultural and archeological zone is a hard-working area where farming remains the economic livelihood of many families. The freshwater springs of Ras el Ain flow through the charming landscape and have been used for irrigation and drinking since Phoenician times; the springs serve the Rashidiyeh refugee camp embedded in the reserve. The springs also provide a habitat for wildlife such as the Loggerhead turtle. May to August is the season for turtle-watching and the beach while early spring and fall are best for bird watching, biking, wildlife photography (authorization required) and hiking. Explore the coastal reserve on foot, by bike or with snorkels and diving equipment. As of this writing, a visitor center is under construction from which guided tours will be provided.

Directions: Take the Autostrade South to the Zahrani exit and follow the signs.
☎ 07-351 341 📱 03-287 211 🌐 www.tcnr98@hotmail.com
🕒 Open year-round. Office hours: Mon-Sat 8am-2pm, Fri & Sat to 1pm

Tannourine Cedar Forest

With around 70,000 cedars, some as old as 2,000 years, Tannourine Cedar Forest is spread over Jabal Mar Maroun and Jabal es Sair between the villages of Hadeth el Joube and Tannourine Tahta. Start your visit at the information center at the main entrance. The 660-hectare forest is stocked with other trees, too, such as cypress, pines and poplars. Its micro-climate harbors a variety of plant species and wild animals including hyenas, boars, squirrels, snakes and bats. Laden with lakes and hundreds of springs, Tannourine is known as the source of the bottled water by the same name.

Directions: Take the Byblos exit off the Autostrade. Veer east towards Aannaya, passing Ehmej. Turn left at Laqlouq and follow signs for Tannourine. The reserve's main entrance is at the village of Tannourine el Fawqa.

☎ 06-500 550   📱 03-679 055   🌐 www.arztannourine.org
🕒 Apr-Nov: 8am- 6pm. Donations welcome

> Tannourine's breathtakingly beautiful Baatara Gorge Waterfall is listed as one of the world's most amazing places by thecoolhunter.net, a popular blog.

The Shouf Cedar Reserve

The iconic Cedar of Lebanon, the national symbol, once covered this land. Most of what remains of the cedar forest is protected at the Shouf Cedar Reserve, which stretches from Dahr el Baidar in the North to Niha Mountain in Jezzine. Within this reserve are three separate forests: Massir Shouf, Barouk and Ain Zhalta on the upper western slopes of the Mount Lebanon chain. There is also an oak forest on the eastern slopes with a panoramic view of the Bekaa. Park rangers keep watch over all. A good starting point for a visit is the Barouk Information Center. From here, arrange for hiking, mountain biking or nature tours. You can hunt for the new man-made pond on the upper slopes, built to encourage wildlife to remain. Plant a cedar tree or just admire the colorful catalogue of flowers, herbs, shrubs and trees. There are 500 species of plants, 32 kinds of mammals and birds galore – over 22 species confirmed residents, the rest migratory or rare.

Directions: Take the Autostrade south to Damour then take road to Beiteddine. Continue past Maasser Beiteddine to Barouk and Ain Zhalta Bmohray center.

☎ 05-350 250/150   🌐 www.shoufcedar.org

Horsh Ehden Nature Reserve

Could this be the Garden of Eden? Located near the village of Ehden, the reserve is situated at an altitude of 1,200-2,000 meters on the upper northwestern slopes of Mount Lebanon and extends across four well-watered valleys. A camp offers outdoor educational activities for children during the week and for adults during the weekend. There's a lot to discover and do: sketch the flora, bird watch, play Name That Tree, even hire a hiking guide. You might get lucky and spot a rare mammal or reptile. There's an incredible collection of plants and wildlife here.

Directions: Head north on the Autostrade, turning east at Chekka towards Amyoun. Drive through Kousba and Toursa, taking the turning to Jbaa. Head east to Ehden.

70-601 601   www.horshehden.org

> Horsh Ehden contains specimens of nearly 40% of all the plants found in Lebanon. Over 1,058 flora and fauna have been recorded to date, 78 of which are recognized as medicinal. As for trees, there are 39 species: 20% of all the Lebanese cedars extant plus Cicilian fir, Greek juniper and the last forest community of endemic wild apples, pear and plum.
>
> A third of all the species of mammals found in Lebanon, many endangered, are found in Horsh Ehden. You might spot the cape hare, the Eurasian badger, the white-breasted hedgehog, the Indian porcupine, the Caucasian squirrel, the striped hyena, the gray wolf or the marbled polecat.

For bird watchers, there's an exciting variety of rare and endangered species: the Eastern imperial eagle, Bonelli's eagle, the Levant sparrow hawk, the Saker falcon, Egyptian vultures, Syrian woodpeckers and storks, just to name a few.

> In case you've been looking for it, the lesser white tooth shrew is endemic to Horsh Ehden.

La Reserve Afqa

Located in El Mnaitra, where apple, cherry, juniper, pine and oak trees grow, this reserve extends for millions of square meters. Situated above the famous cave and waterfall of Afqa, the reserve boasts spectacular vistas punctuated with archeological treasures such as the temples of Ashtarout and Adonis, Yanouh as well as Roman tombs. Your family can explore the nearby grottos at Roueiss, Afqa and Mar Youhanna. Children's imaginations will run wild, inspired by the natural limestone formations, sheared ridges and valleys and plateaus, all with snow-capped mountain peaks as a backdrop. Outdoor opportunities include archery, caving, rappelling, roping and hiking. The reserve organizes sessions in team building, rock climbing and specialized overnight camps for the outdoorsy (and the semi-outdoorsy) to hone their skills. Tents are fully-equipped with beds, pillows, mattresses, electric lighting, toilets and showers (hot water – yes) plus power outlets for cell phones and cameras (see Summer Camps). Open-air living in Afqa surely expands your eco consciousness. The challenge becomes how to incorporate this awareness into urban life.

Directions: Take the Autostrade north toward Meirouba. Follow to Afqa then El Mnaitra (80min). Alternatively, take the main road via Nahr Ibrahim toward Kartaba, arriving in El Mnaitra in 90min.

☎ 01-498 775/6   🖱 www.lareserve.com.lb

> In spring, the air comes alive with sounds of rushing water from the snow melt.

Yammouneh Nature Reserve

Let mythology, mountains and water be your muse! In the northern Bekaa valley, near Deir el Ahmar, lies Yammouneh (little sea) Nature Reserve, site of an ancient sacred spring, Roman temple and lake. Springtime in this beautiful, remote valley flaunts a profusion of gorgeous wildflowers. Picnic at the lake, where, according to legend, the Phoenician goddess Astarte turned herself into a fish when the god Typhon declared war against the heavens. A great campfire story at the very least.

Directions: Drive north to Becharreh, continuing to the Cedars. Drive or climb the path descending to the Bekka Valley towards Yammouneh. (Winter road conditions sometimes necessitate finding alternate routes.)

🖱 www.destinationlebanon.gov.lb

Protected Areas

Aammiq Wetlands

At the Bekaa's western limit lies the largest managed marshland in Lebanon (280 hectares). Home to more than 250 resident species of birds, these wetlands are also an important staging post along the international migratory bird route. The local non-governmental organization (NGO), Rocha Lebanon, organizes activities such as pond dipping, insect collecting, bird watching and guided nature walks as part of a conservation initiative aimed at getting school-aged children involved.

Directions: From Beirut take the Damascus Road toward the Bekaa. Before Chtaura, turn right at Kab Elias. Drive straight for 7km to the wetlands.

www.rocha.org

Bentael Nature Reserve

Pine nut *(snowbar)* and pine cone paradise! A typical Mediterranean pine forest, located northeast of Byblos in the foothills of Mount Lebanon, Bentael is Lebanon's smallest nature reserve (1.5 km). It's situated along the flight path of hawks and eagles. To prepare for sighting these glorious creatures, you might want to read up on them before you go. Visits start at one of two entrances, either near the village of Mechehlene or at the upper region of Bentael village.

Directions: From Beirut go north on the Autostrade; take the Byblos (Jbeil) exit. Go 7.5km, passing the villages of Edde and Kfar Mashoun until you arrive at Bentael.

☎ 09-738 330   www.bentaelreserve.org   Open year-round. Daily 8am-5pm

> Founded in 1981, Bentael was Lebanon's first nature reserve. A worthwhile mission for a determined hiker is to find St. John's rock-cut hermitage and chapel.

Jabal Moussa

Above Kesrouan's coast is a mountain steeped in ecological and historical splendor. Bound by two rivers, Nahr Ibrahim from the north and Nahr el Dahab from the south, Jabal Moussa is 6,500 hectares of biodiversity: 83 bird species, seven of which are endangered internationally, and 14 mammal species have been counted along the wooded slopes, including the squirrel, wolf, hyena and hyrax (a distant cousin of the elephant.) Beyond beauty, Jabal Moussa is culturally significant: the Roman Emperor Hadrian's 2nd century decree protecting the forest is inscribed on a stone along a path dubbed Hadrian's incline. Walk this ancient Roman road with your kids, or commit to an organized 7km hike which lasts 4-5 hours and includes optional lunch at a village house. Call ahead to tailor hike difficulty to the abilities of your family.

Directions: There are a few ways to get to Jabal Moussa:

- Beirut – Zouk Mosbeh – Meirouba – Qehmez entrance (50min)
- Beirut – Jounieh – Ghazir – Ghineh – Nahr ed Dahab entrance (1hr)
- Beirut – Jounieh – Nahr Ibrahim – Yahchouch entrance (75min)

☎ 09-643 464   www.jabalmoussa.org

As far back as 117 BC, Emperor Hadrian was known to engage in forest management. Twenty-three stone inscriptions are scattered throughout Lebanon: a few can be found along Jabal Moussa's trails and one is at the American University of Beirut Museum.

i In 1936, the Kesrouan region was named after a native wild peony, the *paeonia kesrouanensis*.

The mountain and surrounding villages of Jabal Moussa have been designated a biosphere reserve, one of about 500 in the world. These are 'living laboratories' for testing and the exchange of information with the aim of finding conservation solutions.

GREAT GRAPE PICKING

Viniculture plays a long and important role in the history of Lebanon. The Roman Temple of Baalbek was a tribute to winemaking. As far back as 5,000 years ago, the Phoenicians tended vineyards and exported wine to ancient Egypt, Rome, Greece and Carthage. Touring wineries is epically family friendly, especially during harvest season, when children can pick grapes and experience first-hand the hard labor and rewards of agriculture.

Lebanon holds the 2010 Guinness World Record for the largest wine glass.

Lebanon is believed to be the place where Jesus performed the miracle of turning wine into water.

Wineries

Ksara

The oldest of Lebanon's wineries, Ksara lies on the site of a medieval fortress. Extensive underground tunnels are testament to a rich history dating back to Roman times, a story waiting to be told. Founded in 1857 by Jesuit priests, Ksara produced Lebanon's first red wine, mainly for religious services. A guided, 45-minute tour takes you into the labyrinth. What kid wouldn't want to explore 2km of Roman caves? Ksara delivers a great introduction to the science, history and process of wine making.

Directions: Take the Damascus Road towards Zahleh. In Ksara, turn left after the Bakery Chamsine.

☎ 08-813 495   www.chateauksara.com

summer: Mon-Sun 9am-6pm (last tour at 5pm); contact for winter hours

Chateau Kefraya

Come and take in the wine-country vibe of this corner of the western Bekaa. We'd like to shake the hand of founder Count Michel de Bustros for tending so tenderly to Lebanon's *terroir* and for creating such a peaceful oasis near a tenaciously unpeaceful border. At Kefraya, you enter a domaine, a proper vineyard complete with castle, but to families, it's first and foremost a welcoming place. Take an appointment to ride the train through manicured vineyards. Walk through four picturesque parks, each named after a famous opera composer. Linger in the showroom and admire the sublime label art, reproductions of Kefraya-commissioned works by Lebanese artists. End the day with a meal at the restaurant, and, for the adults, some wine-tasting.

Directions: Take the Damascus Road, turning right just before Chtaura. Go 25km, passing Kab Elias. Turn left at checkpoint and follow signs for Kefraya.

☎ 08-645 333/444   www.chateaukefraya.com

> **Every spring, the verdant grounds of Chateau Kefraya double as hunting grounds for Easter eggs.**

Chateau Belle-Vue

A boutique winery in the heart of Bhamdoun owned and operated by the dynamic husband and wife team of Naji and Jill Boutros. The onsite library and peace studies center are clues that there's much more than winemaking going on here: Chateau Belle-Vue is about stewardship of the land, the spirit of abundance and giving back to the community. These broad ideals complement the winery's award-winning products which attract an international clientele as well as the appreciation of wine gurus and connoisseurs. Call to arrange a personal tour starting at the new visitor center and tasting room located at the old French embassy property on the outskirts of the village. The vineyards below hug the terraced valley where families gather at harvest time for a fun day learning to pick grapes and much more.

Directions: Take the Damascus Highway to the intersection of Bhamdoun Station and Bhamdoun Village. Turn right off the highway and follow signs to the village. The visitor center and tasting room are on the left, about 1.5km from the exit. If you pass Le Telegraph restaurant, you've gone too far.

03-221 205   www.chateaubelle-vue.com

We heard it through the grapevine that every September, Chateau Belle-Vue welcomes families to the "Big Crush" – a day of *vendage* (picking wine grapes), a delicious Lebanese lunch and watching the bushels of grapes as they are crushed. Contact Jill Boutros jill@chateaubelle-vue.com for more information.

> It's fun to look for the wine labels designed by the Boutros girls when they were little.

Massaya

Here you visit not only a winery, but also an arak distillery. There's so much for the senses: in the tasting room, you can sample olive oil, honey and molasses – the estate's private label production. Pass fragrant rows of lavender to enter Le Relais, the rustic BBQ restaurant in vineyard center. In summer, enjoy an outdoor lunch, where country-style food is prepared by housewives from neighboring villages. In winter, meals are cooked in a fireplace right in front of you. Call ahead for calendar of events. Massaya sometimes hosts concerts in summer and yoga retreats in fall.

Directions: Take Damascus Road to Chtaura. Continue for 5km, following signs for Massaya.

☎ 08-510 135   📱 03-735 795   🌐 www.massaya.com

🕒 Summer: Mon-Sat 8am-5:30pm, Sunday 10am-5:30pm; Winter: Mon-Fri 8am-4pm, Sat & Sun 9am-12pm; closed Sundays in bad weather

Massaya

Farms

La Ferme Saint Jacques

The only *foie gras* producer in the country is located above Batroun on a hill facing the village of Douma. It operates within the monastery of Mar Yacoub, which lies upon Roman and Byzantine remains. Ducks and ducklings are kept at the farm, two minutes away, where the process and pro-duck-tion of *foie gras* is explained to visitors. Call in advance to book a visit.

☎ 06-520 567   📱 03-477 513   🌐 www.lafermesaintjacques.com

The Country Farm

In the valley of Aintoura, nestled in the crevice between two mountains, a long, winding road leads to an authentic gem of a horse farm. Visit the stables or sign up to ride the horses. Either way, kids will love it.

🏠 Aintoura Valley ☎ 09-220 175 📱 03-665 009

> Down on the farm, or shall we say, sanatorium: former TB rehab Bhannes Hospital has a farm on its grounds, complete with pig sty. It's stinky but kids have loads of fun here once they get used to the smell!

"Everyone will tell you his oil is the best." – **Lebanese proverb**

Olive Oil Press

In October and November, head for Btaaboura, Koura to celebrate the olive harvest with an olive-picking day. Don't miss Mr. Joseph Barbar's olive press for a demonstration of how olives are pressed into oil.

📱 03-517 750

> During olive picking and pressing season, Koura is the place to be. It's an important agricultural center in the north, most famous for and very proud of their olives. See if you can identify the different varieties: Baladi, Shami, Ayrouni and Smoukmouki. Taste-test all and pick your favorite.

Deir Taanayel

Taanayel is an institution in the Bekaa Valley. It's a monastery, run by Jesuit priests, with a farm, lake and fields, a place where tall poplars rustle in the slightest breeze, providing cool respite from the valley's sweltering summer heat. It's an oasis for kids to ride bikes, walk around the lake, run about in the forest or commune with the peacocks and domestic animals. Many come for the dairy shop stocked with the Jesuits' own famous milk, cheese and *lebneh*.

Directions: Take Damascus Road to Chtaura. Head toward the Syrian frontier. Taanayel is on the right.

☎ 08-543 101

Eco Accommodations

An eco vacation means traveling in a way that conserves the environment and improves the welfare of the locals; consider this when you book lodgings. A growing number of lodges adhere to green values, offering nature adventures in a sustainable setting. You don't have to rough it – accommodations can be comfortable. Reserve in an authentic lodge or charming/shabby cottage rather than a hotel chain and see how Mother Nature rewards you. Stargazing is just one of the ways.

Tanaïl Eco Lodge
Authenticity in the heart of the Bekaa. This traditional village was built to reintroduce indigenous mud brick architecture to the region. Visitors sleep in an adobe house with authentic furnishings, getting a feel for the rural lifestyle. True to Lebanese style, the experience includes friendly contact with the local community. Operated by Arc en Ciel, which runs three youth hostels in Lebanon and is a member of the Lebanese Youth Hostel association.

☎ 08-544 881   🌐 www.arcenciel.org

Tanaïl Eco Lodge

Mediterranean Forest Development & Conservation Center of Lebanon
A youth hostel near a pristine forest located in the village of Ramlieh in the Aley district, with 22 furnished double bedrooms. Half-board or full-board accommodations. Women from the community prepare and serve traditional Lebanese dishes in the cafeteria. A good place for an informal family reunion weekend, but don't forget to inform 'Tante Mimo' not to expect the Ritz. Inquire about "sky walking" and their other nature activities.

☎ 05-280 430   🌐 www.afdc.org.lb

Camping Douma

A real wilderness lodge in the middle of a virgin forest. The camp center rents tents that accommodate up to eight people. Expect basic amenities: toilets, bathroom and kitchen. While here, visit Douma, which is not only a beautifully-preserved village of red-tiled roofs, but also a walker's paradise.

03-697 738   www.doumaclub.com

ECOvillage

To stay at the ECOvillage is to be immersed in a real, eco conscious lifestyle. Choose to sleep in the mud huts or tree houses. Eat organic meals, learn about the environment and help out on the farm. Fill the day with organic farming, fishing, hiking, swimming, and rock climbing. Wind down in the evenings with some yoga or tai chi, under the setting sun. Kudos to the passionate and eco minded Khatib family in Dmit Chouf for this admirable endeavor.

05-924 151   03-381 733   www.ecovillagelebanon.com

Orange House

Relaxing bed and breakfast located in the middle of an orchard in Mansouriya, South Lebanon. Run by 'eco hero' Mouna el Khalil, who with Habiba Syed has turned a nearby beach into a sanctuary for nesting sea turtles. Should your family visit in June, you'll observe about 75 turtles emerging from the sea to lay their eggs in deep sand. Return four months later to witness the spectacle of hundreds of just-hatched baby turtles making a dramatic run for the sea. This awesome show beats the National Geographic channel any day.

orangehouseproject@gmail.com   www.orangehouseproject.com

Al Kwakeh Eco Lodge

Near Hermel, Bekaa, you can sleep in one of three traditional village houses powered by green technology and run by a group of local women who want to make the area a destination for responsible tourism. Cozy-up by the mud chimney, snuggle into traditional Bedouin bedding made from goat hair, count the grains in the juniper wood ceilings and feel the responsible tourism.

70-359 659   www.tarhal.org

Stay at the Bazerji's charming Bed and Breakfast with individual cottages in traditional Lebanese style nestled into a green valley just below Beiteddine Palace in the Shouf. Rolling hills of olive groves and infinity pool make for a relaxing getaway. 03-652 888

"The heart of nature soothes the heart of man." – **William Wilsey Martin**

Eco Experts

Consider consulting local experts – they can connect you with a group tour or customize your own outing. Organized packages can be so convenient for newbies and families.

Liban Trek

Main focus is hiking, trekking, cultural tours and alternative travel, both in Lebanon and abroad. Additional activities include cross country skiing, amateur caving, rappelling and green classes. Liban Trek's goal is to promote rural tourism and to delineate paths for the Lebanon Mountain Trail (LMT).
☎ 01-329 975   03-291 616   www.libantrek.com

TLB Destinations

Known for off-the-beaten-path travel experiences throughout the Middle East. Specializes in hiking, trekking and adventure as well as cultural and pilgrimage trips. Tailor-made treks follow the LMT from top to bottom. TLB also lists educational tourism, family tourism, agro and eco tourism among their offerings.
☎ 04-419 848   www.tlb-destinations.com

Esprit Nomade

Rural eco tourism operator aiming to promote Lebanon's natural and cultural heritage. Organizes weekly trips tailored to private groups. Activities include hiking, trekking, rural tourism, mountain biking, camping, night fishing and more.
☎ 09-933 522   03-223 552   www.esprit-nomade.com

Cyclamen

Responsible-tourism operator organizes events that combine theme programs, botanical tours, agro tourism, pilgrimages and outdoor activities. Arranges stays in local guesthouses. Specializes in customized school trips and outings adapted for the mentally disabled.

☎ 04-419 848 or 04-414 697   🌐 www.tlb-destinations.com

Vamos Todos

An eco tourism club for nature lovers. Organizes the standard outdoor activities: hiking, biking, caving and climbing.

☎ 09-635 145   📱 03-561 174   🌐 www.vamos-todos.com

Byblos and Beyond

This relative newcomer to the scene offers interesting itineraries around the country. The company owner worked for TLB Destinations before venturing out on her own.

☎ 09-540 857   📱 03-912 205
🌐 www.byblosandbeyond.com

T.E.R.R.E. Liban

An NGO protecting Baabda Forest, the forest nearest Beirut. It organizes tours and eco activities concerning the conservation of this natural area. Authorized by the Beirut municipality, the company also organizes group visits to Beirut's Pine Park.

☎ 05-923 060 or 05-923 060   🌐 www.terreliban.org

Does anyone in your family want to get involved in protecting the environment? You can become a member, volunteer or even an activist with the organization, Greenpeace, **which helps protects the Lebanese environment under the campaign slogan, "Defending our Mediterranean Sea."**

☎ 01-361 255   🌐 www.greenpeace.org

Hiking on
the Lebanon
Moutain Trail

> "Only when the last tree has been cut down.
> Only when the last river has been poisoned.
> Only when the last fish has been caught.
> Only then will you find that money cannot be eaten."
>
> – **Cree First Nation prophesy**

Lebanon Mountain Trail Association

Dedicated to conserving and promoting the Lebanese Mountain Trail (LMT) and enhancing economic opportunities for rural residents by promoting responsible tourism along the trail.

www.lebanontrail.org

Checklist for Hiking without a Hitch

- Comfy, solid walking shoe or better yet, hiking boots – no sneakers!
- Water – bring plenty
- Sunscreen and sunglasses
- Hat
- Backpack with a change of clothing
- Toilet paper (preferably biodegradable)
- First aid kit
- Food: sandwiches, fruits, snacks, etc.
- Map and compass (if wandering off-trail or unaccompanied by guide)
- Flashlight

Everyone's talking about the LMT. It's the first trail of its kind, linking Lebanon's old hiking paths with new ones to unite the country. Beginning in the North at the village of Qbaiyat, the trail continues through a total of 26 villages along a 440km (275 mile) path ending in the South at Marjayoun.

> "In summer, the song sings itself."
>
> **William Carlos Williams**

Summer Camps

Summer camp is essential in Lebanon because school is out for three, long, hot, lazy months. Choosing the right camp goes a long way toward organizing surplus leisure time and making it memorable. Camps can be grouped into three categories: day camp at beach resort/country club, day camp at school yard or college campus and sleep-away camp. In terms of management, some camps turn to specialized companies. Other camps rely on seasoned educators to run their businesses; still others are an extension of the school program. Most sleep-away camps are run by nature enthusiasts who design programs to their personal satisfaction. Consider first the kind of activities that suit your child and the amount of time he or she can comfortably spend away from home. Summer Camp season is generally July and August.

DAY CAMPS

...at schools

Broumana High School
With nearly 140 years of service as a school and seven as a summer camp, Broumana High School is Lebanon's premier boarding school. Its splendid setting atop a verdant mountain in the resort village of Broumana with lots of green space, picturesque views of Beirut and fresh air attracts an international clientele. Expat Lebanese from abroad and families from neighboring Arab countries as well as locals sign their kids up for either the day camp or boarding option. Accommodates nursery-aged children to 15-year-olds in four or seven-week sessions, weekdays from 9am-2pm with an outing every Thursday. Also offers two six-week academic sessions: the first in math and Arabic or French and the second in SAT I, physics, biology, chemistry and algebra I & II.

Broumana 04-960 430 ext. 447 03-285 176 www.bhscamp.com

Notre-Dame de Jamhour
Located in the hills above Beirut, Jamhour is a Jesuit school reputed for its academic rigor. In summer the Centre Sportive becomes a sports camp for ages 6-12 with well organized activities. Parents are invited to an end-of-session spectacle. Downside: there's a waiting list with priority going to Jamhour students, alumni and members of Centre Sportive, which is not only a school facility but also a private country club.

Jamhour 05-924 133 www.ndj.edu.lb

Lebanese American University
LAU offers three programs for ages 5-12. There's the classic summer camp with an endless choice of activities, some of which are cooking, music, dance, basketball, yoga, chess, art, swimming, storytelling and hip-hop. Then there are two specialized programs: Little Engineers focuses on technology and building skills while Little Leaders integrates leadership and entrepreneurial skills with budget management and creative thinking. Instructors are LAU students. Group ratio is five students for every instructor and monitor. Camp sessions run over six weeks with the flexibility of attending from one to all six weeks.

Koreytem 01-786 456 ext. 1390

O.A.S.I.S.

Well-established program operating under the umbrella of Collège Mont La Salle, O.A.S.I.S. stands for Organisation des Activités Sportives, Intellectuels et Sociales. Operates at four campuses: Collège Mont La Salle in Ain Saade, Antonine International School in Ajaltoun, Ecole Antonine de La Paix in Zahleh and Notre Dame des Pères in Hasroun.

Ain Saade 01-888 195

American Community School

Summer camp here is called Sun 'n' Fun and takes place throughout the urban campus of ACS, both inside and out. From pottery to English composition, the program offers a nice variety of courses within an educational and artistic framework.

Ain Mreisseh 01-374 370 www.acs.edu.lb

American University of Beirut All Sports Summer Camp

For kids aged 6-16 who are serious about sports, this well-structured program takes place at AUB's new state-of-the-art multi-sport facility. Develops athletic skills and sportsmanship through competition and structured games. Coaches provide instruction in basketball, football, tennis, hip-hop (for girls) and swimming. Campers are grouped by gender, age and ability. Weekdays 8:30am-1:30pm in sessions of three weeks but one-week and one-day passes are available. Tuition includes four t-shirts, a cap, a daily snack, drinking water, a medal of participation and a written evaluation of your child's skills. Daily awards for outstanding play, sportsmanship and improvement.

AUB Hostler Center 03- 622 855 tmousally@ic.edu.lb

Wellspring's Summer Language Program

A private "learning community" located near the National Museum, Wellspring has a child-centered philosophy which contrasts with the prevailing culture of stress predominant in the official curriculum. Wellspring offers a daily four-hour summer academic program to strengthen English and Arabic language skills. Priority is given to their students.

Mat-haf 01-423 444

"Sun is shining; the weather is sweet. Make you wanna move your dancing feet." – Bob Marley

...for the very young

Les Citronniers
A nursery school *par excellence* located in a grand old Lebanese house with garden and playground. Every detail in the school attests to director Marie-Claude's experience and dedication as an early childhood educator. The summer program accepts children aged 2 months-6 years. Camp runs weekdays 7:30am-3pm and includes breakfast and a nutritional hot lunch. Outdoor activities include water play and sand boxes; indoors kids draw, paint, dance and sing.

🏠 Achrafieh ☎ 01-327 402 💻 www.garderielescitronniers.com

Lebanese Montessori School Summer Program
LeMonts, as it is known, offers a bilingual program (French and English) which incorporates the methods and materials of Montessori in a more relaxed manner for the summer. Children can attend the full seven-week session or the abbreviated one-week version. The day starts early, at 7:30am, and ends at 3pm, with lunch and snack included. Sample activities are music, culture and geography. The focus is on academics, with a weekly theme to make learning fun through games, movement, cooking and swimming. Great location, just off a tranquil downtown square.

🏠 Saifi Village ☎ 01-971 490 💻 www.lemonts.net

Dents de Lait
Dents de Lait (baby teeth) is an established nursery that operates like a business enterprise with franchise opportunities. Markets itself as an "institute" with a Looney Tunes-esque motto: "Serving happiness". Camp for ages 1-7 means a choice of franchise locations from Bamboo Bay and Pangea Beach in Jiyyeh to the Printania Hotel in Broumana. Take your pick.

🏠 Koraytem ☎ 01-791 561 or 01-792 787 💻 www.dentdelait.com.lb

Mon Jardin d'Enfant

This well-established French-language nursery school in Gemmayze is popular with Francophone-Lebanese society but is borderline cliquish. The founder, the late Claire Massab, was nursery teacher at Nazareth School and had a children's TV program before going on to establish Mon Jardin d'Enfant. Her daughter Nicole currently runs the school. Summer session runs from 8am-2:30pm, with lunch and snack included. One day of the week is reserved for excursions. Activities include the study of Spanish for 4 years and older, plus archery, pool games and more.

Gemmayze, Rue Gouraud 01-564 198 03-356 555

Happy Tots Summer Camp

This group keeps tots happy by taking them out on short daily outings in addition to full-day excursions to water and amusement parks and nature trips to mountains and beach. The six-week camp runs five days a week from 8:30am-3:30pm and longer on Monday, excursion day. Camp concludes with a farewell party. For ages 3-14.

Koreytem, Madame Curie Street 01-786 286 03-747 099
www.happytotscamp.com

Rainbow Nursery

Affiliated with the Armenian Evangelical High School, the summer day care program for ages 1-8 runs 6:45am-5:30pm. Expect sports, music, crafts, dance, French, English, videos and educational games. Kids get lunch and dessert.

Clemenceau, Mexico Street 01-749 364
www.rainbow-nursery-Lebanon.com

Innocent Minds Garderie

Montessori-based pre-school founded by Mrs. Maha Sabbagh, a certified Montessori teacher who trained in London. The program aims to develop a child's personal, social, physical and language skills by learning through play. Activities include art, music, language, science and even cooking. Parents can monitor their kid's progress daily—the school has installed class cameras so parents can view their children on-line. Hours are 8:30am-3pm. For ages 2-6. Located off Bliss Street next to the International College.

Hamra 01-360 026 03-056 976 www.innocentmindsgarderie.com

Hand in Hand Nursery

Summer program with two outings per week. Monday, Wednesday and Friday kids stay at the nursery campus to play in the pool and activity rooms. For children aged 2-5. For each age there's a specific program from yoga to art and crafts. Weekdays 8am-2pm.

🏠 Tallet el Khayyat ☎ 01-786 478 📱 03-189 399
🌐 www.handinhandnursery.com

Learn & Play Children's Center

For ages 1-6, fun includes outings to Oceana Beach Club, Friday dress up days and festive theme lunches such as Pizza Day, Salad Day, Ice Cream Day and Fruit Salad Day. Sounds like a recipe for happy campers.

🏠 Ramlet el Baida ☎ 01-843 002/003 🌐 www.learn-and-play.com

... at beach resorts and country clubs

La Marina Dbayeh

Since 2006 Enfants du Soleil has offered sports, educational and cultural activities at the yacht club on the marina. Generally runs from July to September in either four or eight-week sessions. Children are grouped by age: Club des Petites (ages 3-5), Club des Enfants (ages 5-7), Club des Enfants 2 (ages 8-10) and Club des Ados (11 and older).

🏠 Dbayeh 📱 03-778 203

> **Enfants du Soleil** specializes in entertainment and animation for kids. The company runs four summer camps in Lebanon: Mtayleb, Bel Horizon Country Club, Evangelical School and La Marina Debayeh. 📱 03-778 203

Kids Club Summer Camp at Mövenpick Hotel & Resort

Kids aged 4-12 swim, dance, flip, sing, create art, play tennis, basketball and soccer and more in a luxury resort atmosphere.

🏠 Raouché ☎ 01-869 666 ext. 8785
🌐 www.movenpick-beirut.com

Water Nation Summer Camp

What a glitzy waterfront location for a summer camp! Brand new, this water sports camp overlooks the yachts of Zaitunay Bay. In two-week sessions from July to September Water Nation offers instruction to kids aged 9-16 weekdays from 9am-1pm, with snack included. Show up with bathing suit and towel; everything else is supplied. With sailing, snorkeling, Scuba diving, water skiing, fishing trips, field trips, biking, road safety and kayaking, who can say Beirut summers are boring?

 Zaitunay Bay, Beirut   01-379 770   03-204 455   www.waternation.com

Les Creneaux

Affiliated and conjoined with Nazareth, the private Catholic school near Sodeco, Creneaux is a private health club. Its X-factor is a roof-top swimming pool, an indoor tennis court and access to the school's grounds which include basketball courts and playgrounds. Creneaux's summer camp program caters to children aged 4-15. Focus is mainly on sports: swimming, tennis, ping-pong, soccer, rope climbing, cycling and more. Friday field trips include rafting, sailing and mountain climbing. Camp days begin at 8:30am and end at 2:30pm except on Fridays which run until around 5pm depending on the excursion.

 Achrafieh, near Sodeco   01-615 577   Les-Creneaux

Minicamp at Coral Beach Resort

Since 2001 founder and director Martin (Mini) Mughargil has run an eight-week summer program for kids aged 3-10. The program offers a full range of activities from sing along to story time, art, dancing and water activities for toddlers to swimming football, fishing, "American Frisbee", hockey and handball. Every Friday there is an optional outing.

 Beirut, Coral Beach Resort   03-088 908   www.minicamp.me

Deir el Kalaa Country Club

Serene surroundings and lush Beit Mery location with breathtaking mountain views. Summer camp here is managed by The Two Clown Club, a company specializing in animation and education for ages 2-12. Swimming is standard, but what's refreshing is that each summer there's a new theme: in 2011 it was ecology. A good way to keep returning kids interested. No boring stuff here!

Beit Mery   04-972 988

Mechref Club

Located above Damour, within the confines of the planned suburban community of Mechref Village, camp is special here with its offerings of horseback riding and polo. The program is held at the village's private club and targets the 4-12 year-old crowd.

Mechref   01-707 036   03-877 567   www.mechref.com

Delb Country Club

The weather is cooler and fresher in the foothills of Bikfaya, a verdant village in Metn. The Delb Country Club runs a summer camp with sports galore including dance, football, basketball and swimming. Participating in this down-to-earth, family-geared organization makes great sense if you are summering in this neck of the woods. For children 3-12.

Upper Bikfaya   04-985 460   03-424 970   www.delbcountryclub.com

Golf Club of Lebanon

Yes! Lebanon actually has a golf club. It was established 75 years ago and hasn't really significantly upgraded since, which is the secret of its charm. At this lush oasis located near Beirut airport, expect to find an 18-hole 72 par golf course, fully-equipped tennis center, six-lane swimming pool, diving tanks and a separate children's pool. There's also a playground by a wooded area. The Club hosts a summer camp for kids from the end of June to the end of August. Alternatively, check out the club's private lessons in tennis, golf and swimming.

Ouzai, Bir Hassan   01-826 335/6/7   03-609 412   www.golfclub.org

Many other country clubs, the following included, offer summer camp programs to members and their guests; some welcome non-members.

Al Yarze Leisure Club Yarze 03-346 346
Batroun Village Club Batroun 06-744 333
Bel Horizon Country Club Adma 09-851 310 or 09-853 310
Cap sur Ville Country Club Dekwaneh 01-690 690
La Collina Country Club Rabieh 04-524 584
Country Lodge Bsalim 04-710 502
Faqra Club Faqra 09-300 600
Jeita Country Club Jeita 09-214 111
Mtayleb Country Club Mtayleb 04-419 630
Pineland Resort Hammana Valley 05-380 000
Spring Hills Country Club Mar Roukoz 01-681 242
The Leisure Club Deek el Mehdi 04- 920 921
The Private Club Horsh Tabet 04-920 921
West Bekka Country Club Kherbet Kanafar 08-645 601

...offering specialized programs

Buddha Club

Thirty two years of experience in the martial arts and in sports ranging from tennis and gymnastics to swimming. For children aged 3-17. Weekdays 9am-1:30pm. Bus transport available.
Adma 09-222 000 or 09-855 854 www.bouddahclub.com

Neos Kids

This cultural and educational excursion company is the brainchild of Nour Farra Haddad, archeologist, anthropologist and mother of two. Call for the next didactically engaging summer offering.
Sin el Fil, Pasteur Street 03-733 818

Dolphins Junior Club

With no fixed location, this summer camp is based on the premise that children get enough of routine during the school year and so appreciate a break from it during the summer. A bus scoops up your child from your doorstep and heads off for a fun excursion in a different place every day, be it Waves, Sharewood Camp, Janna Beach, Dream Park or out on a boat, for a mountain picnic, etc. Runs for eight weeks with a flexible sign-up package that also accommodates one-shot participants.

03-701 402   www.dolphinsclub.net

Et cetera . . .

Here's a specialized teaching consultancy company that runs a program to help with summer school homework. Monday through Wednesday, the day is divided into academics, art, book club, educational games and guitar. Every Thursday it's about fun in the sun at the Riviera Beach Club, lunch included.

Manara, El Bahren Street   01-735 841   71-579 262   www.ectlearning.com

Advanced Soccer Academy

If your kid is dreaming of becoming the next Beckham, this soccer training institute may be his or her big chance. The summer program goes from end of June to July.

Sakiet el Janzeer   03-081 819   www.asa-leb.com

Hoops

Jassem Kanso opened Hoops in 2001 with the mission of giving Lebanese youth the opportunity to discover basketball as a discipline and to provide professional training. Now numbering three branches, Hoops is located in a huge hanger that houses a professional-size basketball court and soccer court. During the school year, it's the site of weekend training courses. In the summer, Hoops runs two summer camp programs of three weeks each starting end of June. Open to children from 4-15, the program includes not only basketball but football, badminton, taekwondo, gymnastics, dance and swimming. And every Friday is trip field day.

Antelias, Beirut, Hazmieh   04-411 515, 01-454 586 or 05-454 511
www.hoops-club.com

This just in: Lebanese All Star basketball player Fady Katib and partners have signed to open a professional sports training facility, slated to open in Hazmieh by 2013.

SLEEP AWAY CAMPS

Rockwood

Rockwood is Lebanon's Woodstock, without the funny business. Run by Rock'n Bach Music School, this week-long sleep away experience on a private mountain campsite in Achkout serves as a great introduction to the arts for kids 8-18. Exposure to music, art, carving, painting and drawing gives kids a chance to decide which art field they would like to pursue more in depth. Mornings it's art class; afternoons are filled with DJ or live performances.

Achout ☎ 09-850 330 🌐 www.rocknbach.net

Les Elfes International

Swiss-sponsored summer camp hosted by Aux Cimes du Mzaar hotel in Lebanon from July to September for ages 8-18. Program is designed to be educational, fun and relaxing in Lebanon's premier alpine setting. Kids take French and English lessons and participate in activities from hiking to tennis.

Faraya ☎ 09-341 002 🌐 www.leselfes.com

Nature Land

High adventure on 10,000m of wooded grounds at an elevation of 900m. Accommodations range from wooden bungalows to Bedouin tents. In addition to hiking, tree climbing, archery and more, there are special events such as Teambuilding and Leadership Day as well as Traditional Country People Day: a half-day on the farm, milking cows, gathering chicken eggs and such. Visits to Sohat's water plant at Falougha.

Bzebdine ☎ 01-902 538 📱 03-784 246 🌐 www.nature-land.com

Camp Rage

Guess they mean their camp is all the rage – colloquially speaking we hope. This professionally-run, 14-day camp at the Laqlouq resort is held in July. It's all about the beautiful mountain setting and the outdoors. Daily horseback riding, rafting on the Assi River, archery, climbing, biking, hiking and caving. Organized camping under the stars with bonfire and karaoke for children 7-18. Full-board accommodations at Nirvana Hotel included.

 Laqlouq 03-927 030

Sharewood Camp

Here in Robin Hood country, an orchestra of chirping crickets and the fragrance of pine trees fill the air. Natural mountain boulders offer their shoulders for rock climbing. Kids swing through the air from tree to tree and take refuge in colorful tents. A horse life-size chess set, ping pong table, wooden balance beam, swing set and monkey bars are just some of the simple outdoor diversions. Open since 2000, Sharewood runs not only specialized summer camps for kids; it also accommodates families for weekend getaways or just for Sunday lunch.

 Mar Moussa 03-294 298 www.sharewoodcamp.com

Souraty Centres de Vacances

Family members Violette, Nagy and Elie Souraty run a summer camp that has become a family tradition. In beautiful Faqra, the camp offers a multitude of activities including hand crafts, sports, "expressive arts", music, multimedia, computer and tourism. Two sessions accommodate ages 6-14. All counselors are certified.

 Faqra 01-811 307 03-865 091 www.cvlsouraty.com

Bzebdine Hidden Valley Ranch

Here you can organize your own summer camp for your kids and their friends, cousins, extended family or any group of your choosing. Campsite activities include horseback riding, paintball and caving. Restaurant with open buffet on Sunday.

 Bzebdine, Metn 05-360 863 03-339 370

La Reserve Afqa

The aim of La Reserve is "to instill in young people ... an awareness of the fragility of our own eco system and to guide them towards a respectful approach to nature," so there's a bigger plan at play here than just having fun and staying busy (see Nature). In winter there's snow survival camp, but in July and August special nature and basketball camps include such activities as mountaineering, hiking, trekking, and rappelling. Sessions in teambuilding and rock climbing aim to strengthen outdoor skills as well as character.

Afqa 01-498 775 03-727 484 www.lareserve.com.lb

Summer Camp Batroun by Nadine Tawil Abou

Spending summer overlooking the sea in Batroun, making new friends and sleeping in a charming old house is a great opportunity for children. Former art teacher and camp organizer Nadine supervises small groups of children aged 8-12 as they discover rural culture and the local village traditions, including jam and cheese making and milking cows. Besides the usual sports, arts and crafts, there are excursions to Rashana, Basbous and Jbeil to appreciate the work of local craftsmen. Memorable experiences such as these create the basis for nostalgia in kids.

Batroun 03-366 000 @ nadinea1@hotmail.com

"Being a child at home in the summer is a high-risk occupation. If you call your mother at work thirteen times an hour, she can hurt you."

— **Erma Bombeck**

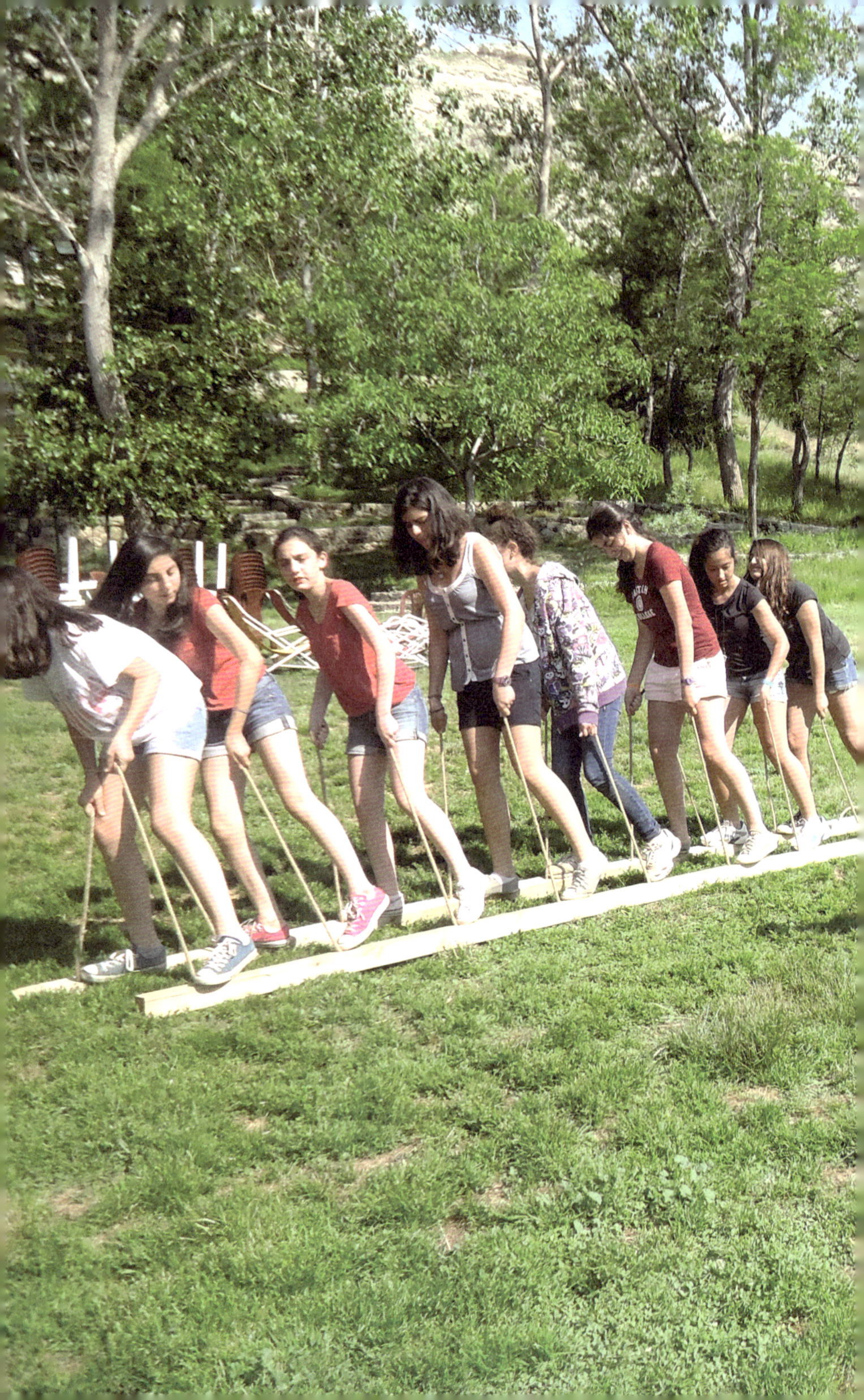

Camp Rage,
Laqlouq

> "On the beach, you can live in bliss." **Dennis Wilson, Beach Boy**

Beach Bliss

Lebanon is blessed with 225km of uninterrupted Mediterranean coastline and over 300 days per year of sunshine. So, yes, most of the time, Life's a Beach, though sitting in traffic to get to the beach feels a lot like the other b-word. In Lebanon, the beach can mean a private resort, a beach club, a free public beach, a marina or even a seaside pool. Here's the difference between clubs and resorts: resorts are open to all but charge an entrance fee. Clubs are restricted to members and their guests. The Mediterranean provides a sublime backdrop for all fun family activities: swimming, fishing, sun bathing, beach clubbing, water skiing, sailing, jet skiing, yachting, alfresco dining and lots more, depending on the beach. Beirut's a 'beaut' for sneaking in a lunchtime-sunbathing session because city beaches are so close by. If you have all day, however, choose a destination: north or south? Sandy or pebbly beach? No two beaches are alike – the beach ball's in your court.

BEACH RESORTS

Beirut

Saint George Yacht Club

The faded glory of mythic Beirut is embodied in the Saint George Hotel, which is still the classic sunbathing spot for diehards. No one seems to notice that it's shabby and sprinkled with Russian working girls overflowing from the Phoenicia Hotel. Families, singles on the prowl, cuddly gay couples – everybody comes to the Saint George. Though the hotel itself remains closed and today is most commonly referenced as the sight of the 2005 assassination of the prime minister, the Saint George continues to serve urban families because of its proximity to the downtown. The saltwater pool is square and small, but curiously just right in the quirkiest way. You can jet ski or learn to dive at the marina or just hang out in the restaurant and casual beach bar hut. The grass patio is always busy with sunbathers on lounge chairs. Though still a private club, there's no more privacy, as the new Zaitunay Bay Promenade overlooks the goings-on at the Saint George and vice versa.

Ain Mreisseh   03-958 379   www.stgeorges-yachtclub.com

> Did you know that Saint George is the patron saint of Beirut?

Mövenpick Hotel & Resort

Glossy international hotel chain with Swiss roots, this hotel and beach resort lies on the city's gold coast facing the postcard-famous Pigeon Rock. It's an island of luxury and leisure with an amazing outdoor tennis court, commanding sea view, great spa, boutiques, numerous restaurants, pools and a marina, which is home to the Dolphin Yachting Team. Boats for hire, scuba diving and more. Kids like the special Swiss ice cream that is only available here.

Raouché, General de Gaulle Avenue   01-869 666
www.movenpick-hotels.com

Sporting Club Swimming Center

Grungy bordering on the decrepit but members wouldn't have it any other way. This classic Ras Beiruiti hangout, oozing with vintage character, boasts two adult swimming pools, one kids' pool and a small, rocky strip for swimming in the sea. A restaurant overlooking the pool and seaside is a great spot for a sunset *mezze* or a breezy early summer luncheon. Always feels like vacation time here.

Ras Beirut, Manara   01-742 481

Riviera Beach Club

This chi-chi spot, aka Silicone Valley for the preponderance of synthetically-enhanced body parts, is a recently-renovated, state-of-the-art hotel beach club complete with stylish pool, swim-up bar and floating island. Lamenting the fact that the Riviera is her daughter's favorite hangout, one mother was recently overhead saying, "Where did I go wrong?"

Beirut, Corniche   01-373 210   www.rivierahotel.com.lb

Coral Beach Hotel and Resort

Comfortable seaside hotel offering pool and beach amenities to members and their guests. There's a pool just for kids, a playground and a nice summer camp program (see Summer Camps).

Jnah   01-859 000   www.coralbeachhotel.com

La Plage

Synonymous with beautiful, bronzed bodies, this St. Tropez-style beach club is small and intimate. An infinity pool adjacent to a stone-arcaded restaurant and a bar perched on a dock add to the discreet, jet set vibe. Entrance is through a curiously nondescript doorway at the start of the Corniche. La Plage is a posh place to tan, for social climbers as well as for real aristocrats, but not for kids.

Ain Mreisseh   01-366 222

South

Bamboo Bay

White, lilac and spring green set a fresh, crisp tone for this popular family resort which sprawls over grassy, terraced gardens. Park yourself in a pool, a private VIP sundeck or a wooded patio on the sandy seashore. Complete with Jacuzzi, restaurants and a shopping courtyard should you need new flip flops on the spot.

Jiyyeh, Sadia Highway, Barja exit   03-513 888   www.bamboo-bay.com

Lazy B

Weathered antiques and dog-eared books are quirky props at this secluded, sandy beach only 20 minutes from Beirut. Listen to the sound of the waves and the wind rustling through stalks of bamboo grass that sporadically shelter cozy sunbathing coves – these sounds cover the usual beach sounds of children shouting. This resort resonates with nature lovers and so does the natural creek shore line, a landscape unique to this beach. The lush, grassy esplanade reflects in the blue Mediterranean. The adults-only section is a place to bring a book and unwind. A relaxing, quiet paradise.

Jiyyeh, Barja exit   70-950 010   www.lazyb.me

Lazy B

La Suite Oceana Beach Resort

The best things about this beach are its expansive, banana-orchard location, hiking trail, organic vegetable market and children's nursery. Otherwise, it's big and brash with fast-food restaurants. No boho-chic going on here.

Damour   03-191 515   La Suite Oceana Beach Resort

Pangea Beach

The long stretch of sandy beach and large pool at Pangea Beach work well for families. Good seafood at the restaurant also helps. All in all offers quality accommodations with recreational activities. One option is to rent a duplex bungalow chalet for your stay.
 Jiyyeh 07-995 570 Pangea

> There are basic, public beaches, some with golden sand, in Jiyyeh, Tyre and Saida. If you don't mind an eclectic crowd or getting your own drink, you might relax in more ways than one at these beaches because entrance is free.

The Bay of Jounieh

Automobile Touring Club of Lebanon (ATCL)

Sailing into the ATCL, you'd think it was Monaco. With its dramatic mountain backdrop and the glistening lights of the Casino du Liban, this may be Lebanon's most glamorous landscape. International yachters stop at the private club and marina to play a little tennis or watch a race car rally. Kids take sailing lessons here. For members only, but then again in Lebanon invitations are easy to come by. The crowd is the pre-war bourgeoisie of east Beirut.
 Kaslik 09-932 020 www.atcl.org

Tabarja Beach

Built in the 1960s, Tabarja is Lebanon's largest resort. Basketball, volleyball and tennis courts in a relaxed atmosphere.
 Tabarja 09-850 661/2/3 www.tabarja-beach.com

Cyan

Known for its music, dancing and party-beach reputation, Cyan is especially fun for teenagers, who also appreciate the water sports station with kayaks, inflatable rafts, boats and jet skis. Still, the little ones are well-served with two pools, one of which is for toddlers, as well as a water toboggan, kid's games and a trampoline.
 Kaslik 09-223 323 www.cyanbeach.com

Palapas Beach

Overlooking the beautiful Bay of Jounieh, this casual resort with pool, snack and bar facilities has suites, chalets, studios and bungalows for rental. Family season memberships run from mid-May to mid-October.

📍 Tabarja ☎ 09-856-655 🌐 www.palapasbeach.net

North: Byblos

Eddé Sands

Pink, purple and posh, Eddé Sands is the beach resort Air France Magazine calls *"la belle phénicienne."* Byblos' fairytale beach exudes luxury and a tropical vacation feel. Attention to detail, from the lounge cushions to restaurant menus, is impeccable. Proprietress Alice Eddé presides over guest relations with grace. Her penchant for gardening is in evidence everywhere on the lushly landscaped grounds. Splurge for a bamboo hut overlooking the pools. And the spa. . . perfect pampering, from Ayurveda and Bach flower therapy to yoga class on the beach. Sandy beach and pools for every age.

📍 Byblos ☎ 09-546 666 🌐 www.eddesands.com

Eddé Sands

Ocean Blue

Chalet rentals by the day or for the season.

📍 Byblos ☎ 09-796 046 🌐 www.oceanbluebyblos.com

North: Batroun

White Beach

Simple pebble beach, low key atmosphere, the kind of place a high-profile diplomat escapes to for an incognito day at the beach. Much appreciated for its family-owned restaurant serving *mezze* and catch of the day, White Beach is also a place for windsurfing, surfing, body boarding, snorkeling, kayaking, sailing and fishing. Sometimes simple just hits the spot.

Thoum, Batroun 06-742 404 www.whitebeachlebanon.com

Pearl Beach

Off the beaten trail, Pearl Beach is a hidden escape disguised as a dinky pebble stone beach. Known as a windsurfer's haven, it's a stone's throw from a unique geological formation: a rock island in the form of Lebanon. Pearl Beach also harbors a tiny, natural rock island with a restaurant perched atop it. Besides eating here, one can indulge in sea sports such as windsurfing, scuba diving, kayaking, snorkeling, fishing, wakeboarding and swimming.

Batroun 06-743 941 www.pearlbeachlebanon.com

Bonita Bay

Located beneath a cliff, this rocky sliver of a beach has a terraced restaurant overlooking the ocean for seaside alfresco dining *à la Libanaise*. Live band on Sundays.

Batroun 06-744 844 www.bonita-bay.com

San Stephano Resort

With a small, sandy beach and pool by a simple marina, this resort has a no-frills hotel with beach chalet-style rooms. There's a well-known diving school on site.

Batroun, Sea Road 06-740 366 www.sanstephano.com

Looking for waves? Blue Bay Beach is a word-of-mouth surfer's spot, a rocky reef where the waves come big and fast. Rough waters are conducive to extreme sports in general, windsurfing included. Check out the friendly rivalry between local windsurfers and boardsurfers: the Pirates vs. the Hurricanes. Gotta go there to guess who's who!

Further North

Las Salinas

Sixty-five miles north of Beirut, on the spectacular Bay of Anfeh is a simple, fuss-free, kid-friendly resort popular with families from Tripoli. There are chalets and cabins to rent or own and a holiday motel to accommodate visitors. The resort offers an amusement center with the latest video games, pool, tennis and hockey tables, indoor volley and basketball courts, a six-lane bowling alley and a summer camp program for kids. At the marina, there's sailing, windsurfing, waterskiing and snorkeling, plus something a little different: an aqua slide and diving pool.

Anfeh ☎ 06-540 970 www.lasalinas.com

BEACH CLUBS AND CHALETS

Rimal

Classic resort designed in the 1980s with children in mind: an amazing pool with a central island and bridge, a sandy playground, cobblestoned pathways for bike riding and a small, landscaped water pond for the resident duck. Chalets on the grass are ideal.

Zouk, Coastal Road ☎ 09-222 104 www.rimalresort.com

Port Emilio

Resembling a Spanish-style tiled village, this chalet complex is connected by landscaped pathways that lead to the pool and beach area. Catering primarily to families in residence and their guests, the complex also incorporates a luxury hotel for tourists and business travelers.

Kaslik, Jounieh Coastal Road ☎ 09-933 300 www.portemilio.com

Aqua Marina

Age-old chalet complex, know to locals as 'Aqua', located in Tabarja, a coastal town 28 kilometers north of Beirut. If you don't own or rent a chalet here you can rent a locker for the season which allows access to the pool, beach and marina. Aqua hosts a kids' club run by Les Deux Clowns educational entertainment group.

Tabarja ☎ 09-855 998 or 09-850 810

Halat sur Mer

Private beach residence with family ambience. Chalets available for purchase or rental, or there's the more affordable cabin option, which equally grants access to both pool and beach. The facility has a marina, a sandy beach and several swimming pools, one Olympic-sized. Onsite restaurant, bars and entertainment facilities.

 Halat 09-477 111

MAIN MARINAS

La Marina JK

Dbayeh is the new waterfront. The Marina is a private club with port for yachts and water sports enthusiasts. With an Olympic-sized pool and children's swimming pool, diving school, two outdoor tennis courts and basketball court, there's plenty to keep every member of the family occupied. La Marina is the site of the Beirut Boat Show and summer concerts.

 Dbayeh 04-418 826 www.lamarinajk.com

Zaitunay Bay

Designed by the American company Steven Holl Architects, this new waterfront marina has a lovely promenade and a long, chic, teak boardwalk lined with smart restaurants, cafés and a few well-selected retail outlets. Open to the general public, Zaitunay Bay also provides open space for regatta events, concerts, exhibitions and celebrations. Facilities will eventually include a yacht club with furnished, fully-serviced apartments.

Beirut Marina

A short walking distance from the Souks, the hotel district and the historic core of Beirut, the Beirut Marina provides mooring for 186 boats.

 Beirut Central District 01-980 650

"The Mediterranean has the color of mackerel . . . you don't always know if it is green or violet, you can't even say it's blue because the next moment the changing reflection has taken on a tint of rose or gray."

– **Vincent Van Gogh**

BEACH ACTIVITIES

Scuba Diving

Diving is a year-round sport in Lebanon since even in winter the temperature of the water never drops below 16°C. The waters are the perfect environment to learn or practice diving skills as marine life is sparse and doesn't detract from concentration. For the more advanced, there's an exciting underwater world to explore: the WW II wreck of the Vichy French submarine, Le Souffleur, off the coast of Beirut, the wreck of the 19th century British vessel, the Victoria, off Tripoli, and, in the waters off Tyre, archeological ruins dating back thousands of years.

- **National Institute for Diving (NISD)**
  Beirut Marina, City Center 01-739 203 03-204 422
  www.nisd-online.com

- **Pure Tech Diving Facility**
  San Stefano Resort, Batroun 03-688 666

- **Atlantis Diving Center**
  Jounieh, Bel Azur Hotel 03-225 686
  www.atlantisdivingcollege.com

- **Calypso Diving Center**
  Beirut, Mövenpick Hotel 03-533 338

- **Dive the Med**
  Safra Marina, Dbayeh Old Road 04-542 365 03-119 002
  www.divethemedclub.com

Sailing

Sailing Together
Laurent Messarra shares his passion for sailing by welcoming guests aboard his cruises to the Turkish coast and the Greek Islands. A word-of-mouth tip: sail the Caribbean with him over New Year's.
🌐 www.sailingtogether.com

Lebanese Yacht Club
Beginner and advanced courses in sailing and off-shore navigation. Training vessels are catamaran, laser standard and Caravelle. The sailing school practices off the shores of Thoum Madfoun, which has clear water conditions and is recognized by the International Sailing Federation and the Lebanese Yachting Federation. Open year-round.
📍 Batroun, Lebanese Yacht Club Building ☎ 70-000 880
🌐 www.lebaneseyachtclub.org

Fishing

Dbayeh Fishing Club
Fishing lessons for all levels and organized fishing trips. A large selection of boats for hire, from yachts to powerboats and fishing vessels.
📍 Dbayeh, La Marina ☎ 03-256 626 🌐 www.dbayefishingclub.com

Before You Go:
- Steer clear of river estuaries, sewage pipelines and coastal factories
- Beware of jellyfish – high season is July and August
- Learn to swim

Let's face it; you can only relax at the beach when everyone in the family knows how to swim. Learning to swim is really worthwhile and can be done at the nearest country club.

Lifestyles Health Club ☎ 01-360 335 and **Les Creneaux** ☎ 01-615 599 are two of the many facilities in Beirut that offer swimming lessons for kids during the winter season.

> "Living in Lebanon can be like riding a roller coaster." **Anonymous**

Amusing Parks & More

Lebanon's diversions are truly diverse, ranging from a cowboy and Indian encounter in Keserwan to a dinosaur village in Ajaltoun and Americana mall-style amusement centers in between. Water parks are numerous and up-to-date since the Lebanese rely on aqua action to get them through the long, hot summers. On the other hand, the Gilded Age still reigns in dilapidated-chic amusement parks. You won't find any big theme parks here, but some find the orderly perfection of Saifi Village reminiscent of Disneyland.

WATER PARKS

Water park season runs May or June to September. Remind the kids to take a dip, not a sip.

Rio Lento

Lebanon's first water park, a family-run business modeled on a water park in Atlanta, Georgia, is not as thrilling or fancy as some other water parks, but is ideal for ages two and up. Children roam freely, laughing, playing and swimming, simply having a great time without constraint. You won't find any "Over 18 Only" signs here, even on the favorite slide, the Sidewinder. In all, there are eight slides, a wave pool (1,200m) and what the Lebanese call a "lazy river" – a slow, winding waterway to float along. The park has added land activities for both parents and kids: basketball and tennis courts and a playground for those not in the mood to get wet. Substantial savings if you go in the afternoon. Snack concession offers kids' burger meals at a reasonable price.

🏠 Nahr el Kalb ☎ 04-915 656 www.riolento.com ⏰ Jun-Sept: Daily 9am-7pm

Rio Lento

Watergate

Buccaneer-themed Watergate has a wonderful location, perched on a hill overlooking the Beirut skyline and attached to the five-star Le Royal Hotel. Of its six water slides, the most talked about is the Black Hole in which the rider descends into a dark tunnel before being catapulted into a pool. This park is pricey so come early to get your money's worth. Downside: excessively loud pop music is often pumped through the park and the main pool can get crowded.

🏠 Le Royal Hotel, Dbayeh ☎ 04-555 666 ⏰ May-Sept: Daily 10am-7pm

Waves

At 60,000m², Waves is the largest aqua park in Lebanon. With its picturesque, pine-forest setting in the hills of Metn, Waves feels like a resort, so both parents and kids will find their niche. Tote along water toys from home to keep the little ones occupied in the kiddy pool. Older kids like the Blizzard, an exhilarating slide, and all ages go for the wave pool for which Waves is named. The over-18 crowd heads for the Island Pool to enjoy a drink from the bar. Waves is especially big on hosting events such as weddings and banquets.

Mansourieh 04-533 555 Jun-Sept: Daily 10am-7pm

> Waves' 2,700m² pool is the largest in the Middle East.

AMUSEMENT PARKS

Luna Park

Named for the turn-of-the-century Coney Island amusement park in Brooklyn, NY, Luna Park is Lebanon's oldest — its iconic Ferris wheel survived the Lebanese Civil War. Located at Manara just north of Pigeon Rock, this small park with its carnival booths oozes with 1960s kitsch, which is amusing in itself.

El Manara, General de Gaulle Street

Dream Park

On a mountainside along the road to Faraya, Dream Park is one of Lebanon's busiest amusement parks. Classic open-air rides for all ages, such as the merry-go-round, haunted house and sky drop. Neighboring carting circuit adds value.

Zouk Mosbeh 09-223 817 Daily 10am-10pm

Fantasy World

For the kind of thrills and chills an adventure into Beirut's southern neighborhoods elicits. Classic amusement park catering to the pious. No beer served here.

Beirut, New Airport Road 01-451 186 03-409 444/555

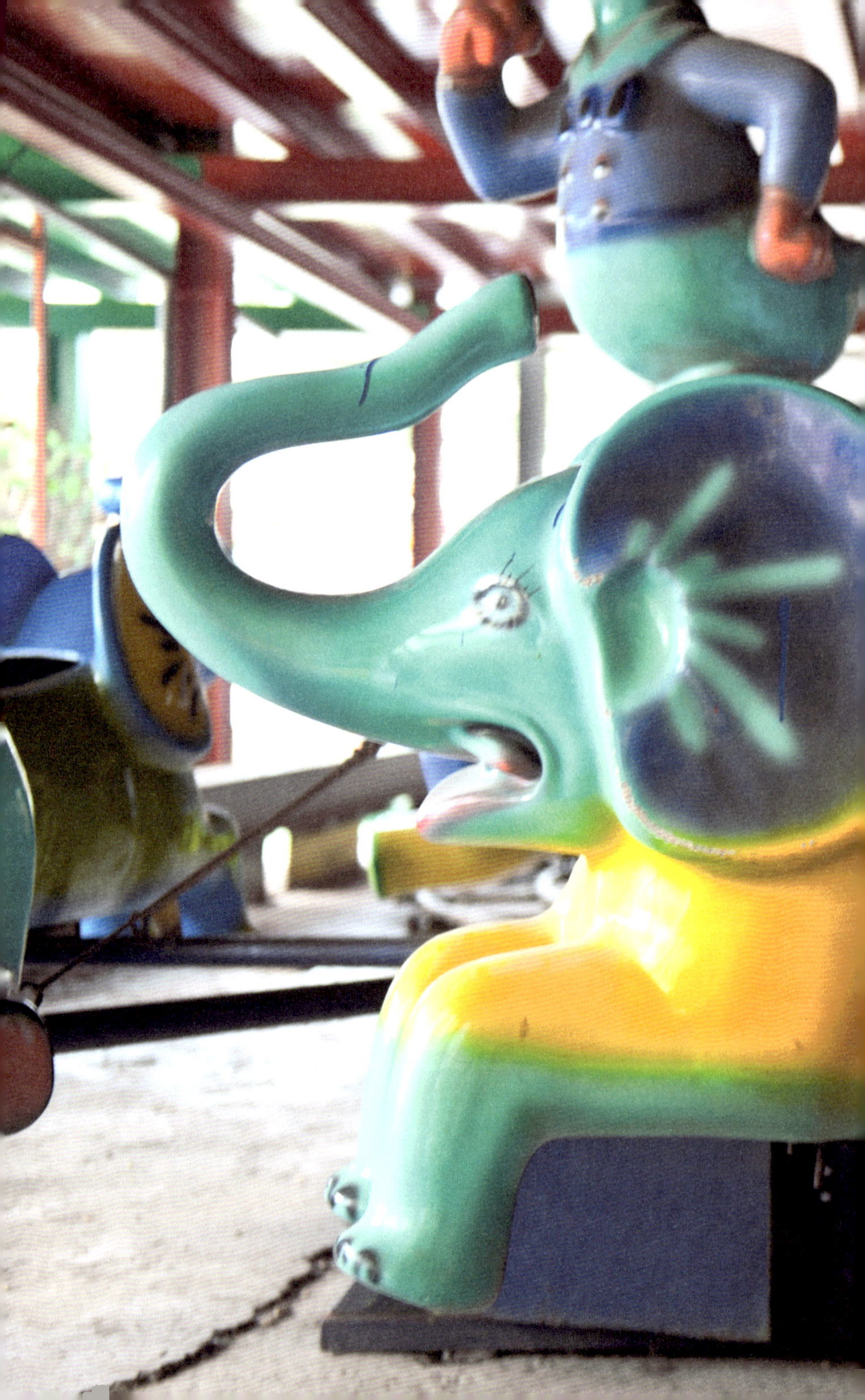

Luna Park,
Beirut

THEME PARKS

Kidzmania

Slated to open in the summer of 2012, this indoor, interactive theme park promises to combine education and entertainment. Designed for kids aged 2-14, Kidzmania will be a replica of a real city with activities based on local culture and society. With over eighty professions to choose from, children will role play in a realistic environment using play currency to learn about earning, spending and saving money. On the blueprint: a Ferrari race track where kids can learn to drive in safety as well as a flight simulator controlled by Middle East Airlines (MEA). Educational day care center for ages 1-4.
🏠 Beirut Waterfront ☎ 01-976 676 🌐 www.kidzmania.com

Kidzmania

Yuppie Park

Probably named for the French *youpie* (hooray) rather than the English 'young urban professional', Lebanon's largest playground has swings, slides, sandbox, see saw, spider climbing wall and a sandy space for kids to let out all their rambunctiousness. Onsite snack concession serves classic kids' fare: nuggets, burgers, etc. Popular venue for birthday parties.
🏠 Ain el Remmaneh, Camille Chamoun Boulevard ☎ 03-406 408

El Rancho

El Rancho is a wild west-style activity center up in the mountains of Ghodras. Families are fond of coming here for the animals, farming, camping and horseback riding. It's Twilight Zone-esque, an Indian village complete with teepees, restaurant and extreme sports in the Middle East sierra – but peerlessly quirky and worthwhile.

🏠 Ghodras, Adma Highway ☎ 09-741 188 📱 70-899 201
🌐 www.elrancholebanon.com

Dino City

According to their website, Dino City "... tells the story of pre history as never told before... for the first time in Lebanon, in the Middle East and maybe in the world... displays the miracle of life in a natural and magical setting based on scientific data." Get over the grandiose pitch and the corny pre-historic-man statue and just let your kid go down the slide.

🏠 Ajaltoun, Main Road ☎ 09-232 316 🌐 www.dinocity-lb.com

Science Village

Located on the grounds of the former Green Fields Park, facing Le Royal Hotel, above the Dbayeh Highway. It's an edutainment facility designed to spark interest in science by engaging kids with hands-on activities. Like a small science museum, it has workshops in physics, chemistry, biology, and the environment. School visits by appointment. Open to the public Saturdays only from 3-6 pm. Moms take note: this is a good place to hold a birthday party.

🏠 Dbayeh ☎ 04-543 129 📱 03-067 035 🌐 www.sciencevillagelb.com

Splash Land

Under new management, the former Splash Mountain bills itself as an "active park for all seasons", with plenty of indoor amusements such as trampoline and wall climbing that are open year-round. Outdoor pool in the summer. Onsite fast food concession is a plus. Money-saving family memberships are available.

🏠 Ain Saade ☎ 04-531 166 🌐 www.splashlandlb.com

MORE

Pit Stop Karting

Feel like burning some rubber? Open since 1995, this venue sports a huge race track for beginners, amateurs and professionals alike. Besides a 10-minute spin, which, by the way, will cost you, Pit Stop also offers training and competition for kids with their own go carts in conjunction with the Automobile Touring Club of Lebanon.

📍 Zouk Mosbeh ☎ 09-219 760 🌐 www.pitstopkarting.com 🕐 Daily 2pm-11pm

Knots and Ropes

The main activity here is walking from tree to tree anywhere from 2-12m above ground on suspended bridges known as accrobranches. Fun, confidence-building and good exercise. Open year-round by appointment only.

📍 Beit Mery ☎ 03-857 403 🌐 www.knotsandropes.net ƒ Knots and Ropes

Knots and Ropes

Hippodrome du Parc de Beirut

Beirut's racetrack is located near a pine forest adjacent to Beirut's biggest park and grandest French Embassy residence (the ambassador's). While we don't condone betting, we do admire the racetrack itself and the beautiful Arabian horses. The annual garden show takes place on these grounds in May, with nice activities and goodies for the kids.

📍 Forêt des Pins ☎ 01-632 515 🌐 www.beiruthorseraceing.com

XTrem Paint Ball

Paintball park with two playing fields: one for speed ball which involves five-member teams and the other a scenario playing field where two teams of ten players each reenact combat.

Dora, City Mall 03-489 191 www.xtrem-paintball.com

ENTERTAINMENT CENTERS

Located in malls or near shopping areas, these centers are a convenient drop-off stop to spare children the boredom of shopping.

Adventure World

Indoor family park with more than 60 games and rides for tots and teens. Located in the Beirut Mall.

Tayouneh, Beirut Mall 01-385 330
Open weekdays 11am-10pm, weekends 10am-10pm

Bateux Rigolo

Your kids can play, dance and work on crafts while you shop at City Mall.

Dora, City Mall 01-905 083 Daily 10am-8pm

Jungle Land and KidsVille

Saturday and Sunday shows to entertain the kids while parents are free to shop until they drop at ABC.

Achrafieh, ABC Mall 01-212 888 ext 2828 Daily 10am-8pm

ZOOS

The truth is, Lebanon has only one zoo. There were others, but they closed and sold their animals to Animal City, a private enterprise.

Besides the zoo, there is an animal rescue and education facility that opens to the public.

It's interesting to note that most foreign workers living in Lebanon can claim better animal exhibition facilities in their home countries.

Animal City

Home to over 45 species, including baboons, ostriches, crocodiles, jaguars and tortoises that have been rescued from the wild and from farms. On Sundays, a boa is taken out of its cage for petting under the careful watch of its keeper. Be advised; this is not the Bronx Zoo; animals are kept in small cages and conditions don't meet international standards. But in Lebanon not even humans can count on regular electricity and water, so what can we expect for these poor animals? Though visitors may have to downplay the urge to call the animal protection agency, Animal City remains popular for its pet shop, photo shop and inflatable castle.

Nahr el Kalb Valley, Zakrit Road ☎ 01-691 316 or 04-930 320 03-280 505
 Animal City Admission Daily 10am-7pm

> Before finding a home in Animal City, Prince the Lion was abandoned by a bankrupt circus.

Animal Encounter

Works like a small zoo, but is really a non-profit educational center for wildlife conservation. With live tours and an outdoor classroom it promotes awareness about species indigenous to Lebanon, including the bear, hyena, jackal and wolf. Animal Encounter also plays an important role as an animal rehabilitation center, rescuing wounded wild animals and nursing them back to health for re-release into their natural environment. Open on weekends to the public and by appointment during the week.

🏠 Aley ☎ 05-558 724 🌐 www.animal-encounter.org

"Be Prepared." Scout Motto

Birthday Bling

IF you're raising children here, the bulk of your child's social agenda will involve the birthday party circuit. It's a phase that starts at pre-school age and peters off by the pre-teens, but not before a final hurrah of DJs and dance parties. Until then, if your weekend is not full of gift-buying and chauffeuring to other kids' birthdays, it will be filled with preparations for your own. It's best to go in knowing that Beirut socialites like to out-birthday each other. Otherwise-reasonable mothers transform into competitive hostesses vying for the most original party favors, over-the-top-entertainment and confetti-colorful buffets – it's what the Beirut birthday bonanza boils down to. So Be Prepared: research your child's preferences, have ideas to pitch, work around a theme and be familiar with birthday party etiquette. With the following information in hand you'll be better prepared to please your child, sidestep the stress and maybe even enjoy the celebration.

ENTERTAINMENT

Event Attack
Looking to hire a fire show and circus? They are Event Attack's specialty. They also supply trampolines, obstacle courses and even a rock band. With their amazing footwork combos and flips, the Break-Dancers Crew delight and astonish audiences of all ages. Hire four or eight and they'll teach party guests the basics of break-dance.
☎ 01-899 499   📱 03-019 019   🌐 www.eventattack.com

Luna Fun
The sky is the limit when you rent a bungee and trampoline. Other large-scale devices such as inflatable rides, electric games and air hockey machines are also available. Luna Fun organizes parties in the garden of your private villa or at their home base in Hazmieh.
📱 03-315 375

Special Events
Planning parties since 1993 with the slogan, "You dream it; we theme it." They propose themes such as a set from the movie *Fame* or a princess tearoom and then deal with the details.
☎ 01-861 700   📱 03-864 971

Magician Samir
Pigeons appear and disappear. Dogs, ducks, turtles and rabbits also implicated.
📱 71-698 681

Cirque du Liban
A customized-entertainment provider with 25 multi-talented animators to choose from. Hire all and you bring the circus to town, including magicians and clowns on stilts.
📱 03-158 039   🌐 www.cirqueduliban.com

Dr. Miki

In a field full of magicians, Dr. Miki is the benchmark against which other performers are measured. In top hat, black tuxedo, bow tie and matching assistant (his wife), Dr. Miki has been entertaining at children's birthday parties for decades. Good for all ages.

Jdeideh, Rawda   01-682 602   03-340 952

Jnoon

Event organizer offering birthday entertainment packages. The basic deal includes two entertainers for face painting, balloon art and puppet shows. Optional arrangements can be made for the cake ceremony piñata, decorative balloons and shows from juggling to gymnastics.

01-547 113   03-606 113   www.jnoon.me

Wishes Come True

Provides entertainment, activities and professional decorating of the birthday venue.

01-561 791   03-922 668

The Two Clown Club

AKA Les Deux Clowns, suppliers of costumed characters to entertain the crowd with performances and workshops. Trained animators set up treasure hunts and direct activities such as "crazy dunkers", acrobatics and Taekwondo demonstrations. Tattoo stand adds to the fanfare.

01-564 198   03-902 589   www.c2c-me.com

Kiki Monkey

Party planners specializing in bouncy castles and inflatable rides. Kiki has an entertainment center, open all week, that your kids can test drive. There's a bungee trampoline, kiddy cars and a café serving arguileh, a thoughtful provision for parents.
☎ 04-715 987   📱 71-898 968   🌐 www.kikimonkey.com

Oh! happy days

Professional party entertainers and organizers. Their boutique headquarters is open for activities and walk-ins.
☎ 01-215 831   📱 70-252 726   🌐 www.ohhappydayslb.com

Tea 'n Apple

Animation and education assemblage fronted by original character Funny Nanny, animator and face painter. Organizes karaoke and theatre theme parties.
☎ 05-462 186   📱 70-839 298   🌐 www.teanapple.com

CONFECTIONS

"All the world is birthday cake, so take a piece, but not too much."

– George Harrison

Cakes

Pâte à Choux

Their strawberry shortcake's the best in town and the *mille-feuille* is amazing.
🏠 Sodeco, Achrafieh   ☎ 01-614 150

Sugar Daddy's Bakery

The cupcakes here look scrumptious but are quite sweet. The carrot cake in particular is super moist and tasty. There are great looking pies, cookies and special order cakes too, including the British sweet, Banoffee.
🏠 Ras Beirut, Koraytem Highway   ☎ 01-787 487   🌐 www.sugardaddysbakery.com

T-Square

Known for specialty cakes that impress. If you can describe it, they can create it. They taste good, too.

🏠 Achrafieh, Sodeco Square ☎ 01-612 058 📱 03-744 128

La Mie Dorée

A gourmet's paradise since 1980. A bite of their La Vie en Rose cake will put a smile on any face, but especially appropriate for children's birthdays is either Le Petit Philippe, a crispy chocolate confection with cream and meringue or Le Carnaval, a chocolate almond cake with crispies. Everything here is delicious and refined.

🏠 Achrafieh, Ghazalie Street ☎ 01-216 730 or 01-202 678 🌐 www.lamiedoree.com.lb

Cannelle

Fine desserts disguised as birthday cakes. One taste instantly transports you to a luxury Relais & Châteaux destination.

🏠 Tabaris, Chehab Avenue ☎ 01-202 169

Cocoa & Co.

Each cookie is a colorful piece of art, almost too pretty to eat. But do eat them – they are scrumptious. And the brownies are the best in town.

🏠 Achrafieh ☎ 01-323 668 🌐 www.cocoa-and-com

Boutique Ladurée

French macaroon specialists come to downtown Beirut. If you are going to splurge on this gorgeous, delicate confection, this is the address. A birthday tea at the shop itself would make for a quaint celebration.

🏠 Foch Street ☎ 01-992 922 🌐 www.laduree.com

Noura

Chocolate lovers swear by Noura, especially their "N" de Noura chocolate cake. Catering is done out of their Sioufi location while cakes, croissants and chocolates are sold at a boutique facing ABC, near Sassine.

🏠 Achrafieh, Salam Street ☎ 01-425 533 (catering) 📱 03-450 111 🌐 www.noura.com

Colorful cookie and cake counter at Cocoa & Co.

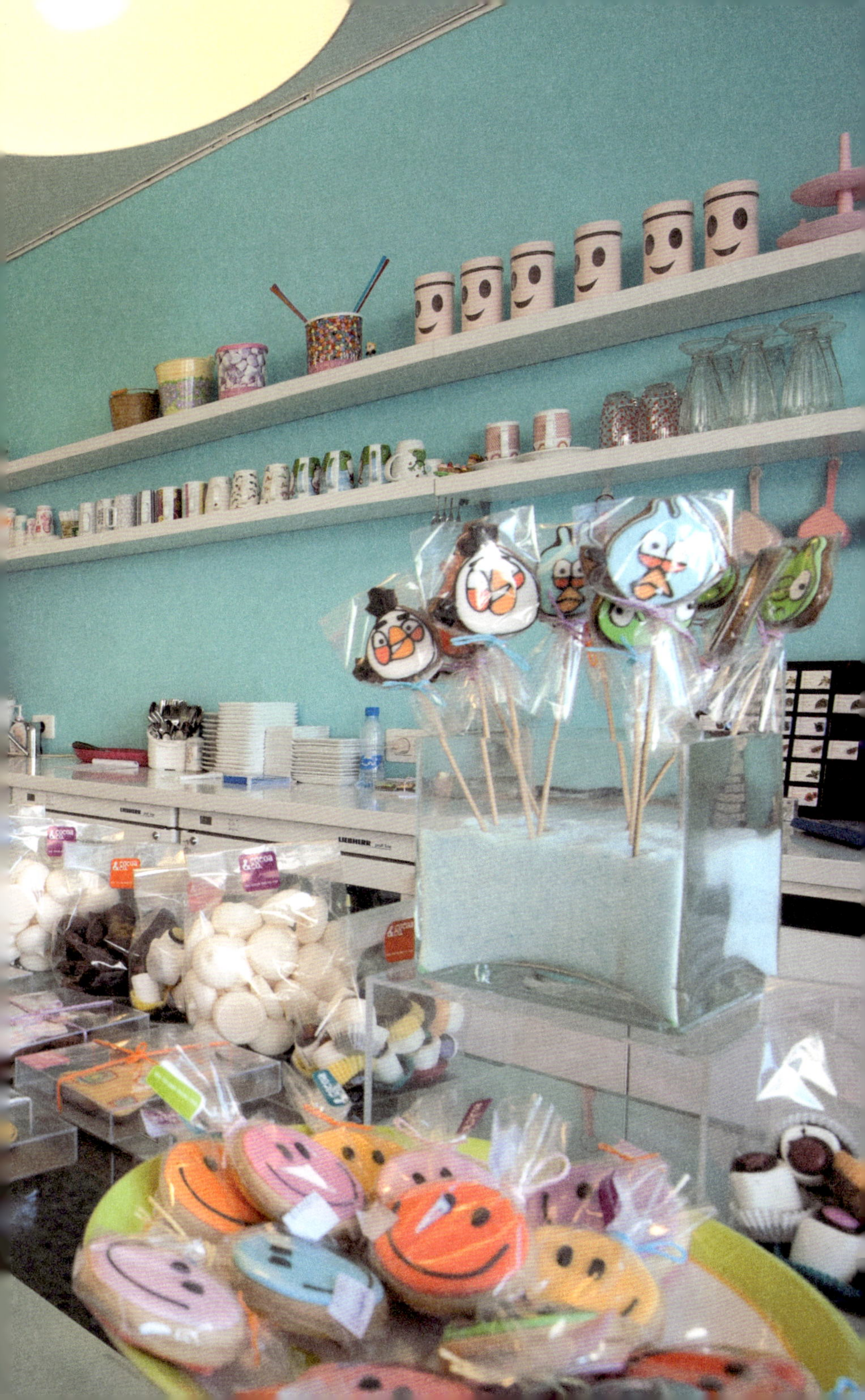
LIEBHERR

Secrets – Hazem Arayssi

Good value really counts when you're ordering in big quantities. Secrets make a great *crème brûlée* served in traditional pottery dishes. By far their most popular birthday cakes are both sponge cakes: the Cortina with profiteroles, and what they call Moist Cake, chocolate cake served with chocolate sauce on the side.

🏠 Koraytem Highway, Ras Beirut   ☎ 01-801 506   🌐 www.secretshazemarayssi.com

Fun Cake

Makes mainly jelly lollipops in many shapes, from butterflies to dinosaurs. A popular party pick is the cotton candy cups in nine flavors and colors, which are said to have a shelf life of 12 months . . . which is a good thing, right?

🏠 Aintoura, Jeita Square   ☎ 09-237 361   📱 03-679 170
🌐 www.funcakelb.com

Special-order Cakes

If you fancy a cake free of gluten and sugar, try Passion For Dessert's **healthy offerings. Hanan el Khatib prepares flour-substitute cakes and tweaks favorite recipes. By advance order only.**

📱 03-022 461   🌐 www.passionfordessert.net

Toumourana

Rana Arayssi Tabbara has turned her kitchen into a bakery selling homemade, custom birthday cakes, cupcakes and desserts "just like mom's" – in other words, the kind you can get away with saying you made yourself. Her specialty is date desserts.

🏠 Koraytem   📱 03-339 333   f Toumourana

Cupcakes

Cup n' Cake

Their light and fluffy vanilla coconut is to die for. Buy a bunch and they'll provide a cupcake stand for display. They make full-sized cakes as well.

Achrafieh, Saint Nicholas Street   01-329 416
03-411 211

The Cupcakery

Beirut's answer to New York City's Magnolia Bakery, the Cupcakery sells all shapes and colors of the vintage dessert: classic, giant, special-order, "topless" and even cupcake pops. Fun flavors include piña colada, banana caramel fudge and "Rebel in Red".

Hamra, Jeanne d'Arc Street   01-752 751   www.cupcakery.org

VENUES

With thousands to choose from, here are just a few suggestions.

Planet Discovery

Children's Science Museum that can be rented out for private functions including fun-filled educational birthday parties. Call to custom plan the party.

Downtown, Omar el Daouk Street   01-980 650/60

Living Colors

Spacious venue with outdoor playground. Indoors, there are interactive games built into the walls for infants and tunnels for those a bit older. The second floor and backyard are particularly suited for birthday parties. Ask about their in-house party planning service and theme options. The trendy teenage club befits the 10-18 year-old set.

🏠 Dbayeh, Main Highway ☎ 04-541 540 🌐 www.liv-colors.com

Niños

This funky lounge for teenagers is an ideal hang out and party place. Popular not only for parties but also for photo shoots, DJ training and dance classes. Nikon directs a photography workshop for teenagers in this space.

🏠 Achrafieh, Sursock Street 🌐 www.ninosclub.com

JouéClub

A birthday party in a toy store? Why not, since JouéClub takes over the decorating and animation at their branch in Verdun. The European toy store chain makes for a colorful backdrop and is perhaps the closest thing in Lebanon to holding a party at FAO Schwarz.

🏠 Verdun, Ain el Tineh ☎ 01-800 897

Fun Factory

One-thousand-square-meter entertainment center offering a wide range of activities from puppet theater and car racing to ceramics. Hosts birthday parties as well as after school clubs and holiday camps, and so is well-equipped.

🏠 Zouk Mosbeh, Joe & Joe Center, Zouk Mosbeh Highway ☎ 09-217 679
🌐 www.funfactorylb.com

Bzebdine Hidden Valley Ranch

Celebrate on a mountain ranch 900m high in the Metn. Here kids can ride horses, feed the animals and play outdoors at a variety of activities including paintball.

☎ 05-360 863 📠 03-339 370 🌐 www.bzebdinehiddenvalleyranch.com

CocoBerry Kids Club
Provides a pleasant venue, especially for toddlers. CocoBerry Birthday Club services organize your child's birthday party from A to Z.
🏠 Rabieh, Barakat Building, Main Road ☎ 04-522 646 📱 03-186 245

TOY AND GIFT SHOPS

"If you can give your child one gift, let it be enthusiasm." – **Bruce Barton**

JouéClub
This European franchise has three outlets across Beirut, in Verdun, Achrafieh and the Beirut Souks.
🏠 Achrafieh, Alfred Naccache Street ☎ 01-320 339
🏠 Verdun Branch ☎ 01-800 898

Purple Dragon
Stylish children's toys and room accessories, books, scooters and fun gift items. And yes, they have miniature dragons, too.
🏠 Achrafieh, Rue du Liban ☎ 01-201 013

Early Learning Center
What a blessing that this British toy franchise now has four branches in Lebanon thanks to Bassam Abdel Rahim and his British wife, Caroline. ELC carries quality educational toys for newborns to 7-year-olds. Shop ELC for arts and crafts supplies as well as clothes and accessories. Locations in Verdun, Achrafieh, City Mall and Dbayeh.
🏠 Achrafieh, ABC ☎ 01-338 777 🌐 www.elclebanon.com

Rooly Booly
Lovely local boutique with a thoughtful selection of well-chosen toys and gift items. Sometimes less is more.
🏠 Achrafieh ☎ 01-218 182 📱 03-290 034

Mazen World

Big selection, including outdoor playground equipment, baby accessories and clothing. The main shop is in Corniche el Mazraa but there are branches in Achrafieh, Dbayeh, Saida and Zouk Mosbeh. And if you had a shop, you'd probably name it after yourself, too.

📍 Mazraa ☎ 01-300 444

ABC Toy Store

Department store shopping with a good-sized toy section from manufacturers around the world. You'll find the classic Lego set or Barbie doll here.

📍 Achrafieh, ABC Mall ☎ 01-212 888 ext. 2229

SPECIAL OCCASION DRESSING

"One should either be a work of art, or wear a work of art." – **Oscar Wilde**

Lola & Moi

Sewing for her twin daughters inspired Rania Tohme to create this cheerful children's clothing label. Her designs mix and match patterns with prints and in colors that evoke the sweetness of a candy shop, and the result is precious and unique. The boutique concept and look have been so successful that the business has been franchised abroad. Imagine the red carpet stars at the Beverly Hills location dressing their starlets to look like little girls in Beirut!

📍 Achrafieh, ABC Mall ☎ 01-212 888 🌐 www.lolaetmoi.com

Plum Kids Store

The result has gotta be upscale and chic when two "It Girls" open a kids' concept clothing store. Understated elegance in the best designer labels for newborns, kids and 'tweens. Accessories, too: high chairs, cribs, strollers, etc. Nice selection of gifts and gadgets, including books, CDs, bikes and scooters. Good taste in evidence here. There's also a Plum concept store for adults at Park Avenue.

📍 Saifi Village, Kanafani Street ☎ 01-976 567 🌐 www.plumconcept.com

Sunflowers

The Sisters Skaff are the sunflowers behind this shop. Their own fun designs and the work of select Lebanese designers are showcased in accessories, bags and clutches, clothes, cute baby stuff, bits and pieces and the Carla Skaff jewelry collection. The baby bibs make fun presents that are always welcome.

Saifi Village, Mkhallasiye Street   01-972 727   www.sunflowersboutique.com

Kidding

Best friends Joanne and Katia opened this adorable concept boutique for outfitting kids aged 2-16. Clothes are hip and trendy with designer labels from Europe and Australia. Kidding commissions Lebanese fashion designers to create one-of-a-kind pieces. Check out the colorful display of funky accessories and vintage novelty items such as the yoyo, water-squirting camera and more. Kidding is small in size but big on stylish merchandising. Free candy for clients and a loyalty card keeps both moms and kids coming back for more.

Achrafieh, Chehadeh Street   01-337 371   Kidding Kids & Tweens

Lollidots

Stylish boutique for kids' clothing (newborns-10 years). T-shirts with cute sayings are a popular item. Lollidots carries a line of personalized gift items, too: for example, a custom monogrammed director's chair would make a unique gift.

Achrafieh, Abdel Wahab el Englizi Street   01-320 902

Les Ateliers de Rififi

Lebanese designer Claudine Mokhbat uses luxury fabrics in her precious couture dresses for children up to age 16. The boutique's lovely pastel decor makes shopping a delight. Open by appointment only.

Achrafieh, Achrafieh Street   03-361 502

Cookie Dough

This shop is a dream, not only for moms on the lookout for luxury clothing and adorable accessories but also for boutique owner Yasmin Agha, who in opening it has realized a lifelong dream. In addition to seasonal collections from around the world, Cookie Dough carries three Lebanese designers: Alia and Sprinkles make special-edition hand bags and Lula provides custom hair accessories. Precious Tales from the Earth silver charms from England complement funky giftware such as "Even my poop is cute"-emblazoned snap suits. A personalized shopping service provides limousine transfer from airport to hotel where select items are available for private viewing, a perk that makes for a steady clientele of royal sheikhas. Not to be outdone, young professional Beirut moms confer Cookie Dough gift certificates via Blackberry.

Clemenceau, May Ziadeh Street 01-364 073 03-907 137
www.cookiedoughbeirut.com

> Portraits of children make souvenirs that stand the test of time.
>
> **Too Cute to Shoot** specializes in the kind of photographic portraiture that families can have fun with.
> 01-652 134 03-638 683 www.toocutetoshoot.com
>
> **Dina Debbas** is known for her classic family portraits that are stylish. A photoshoot in her studio is a great experience.
> www.dinadebbas.com

THEME PARTY IDEAS

Cooking

Kids love to cook and bake. How nice to leave the mess and sticky fingers to someone else's kitchen!

Cocoa & Co.
Celebrate in what may be the cutest professional kitchen ever. Decked out in aprons and monogrammed hats, kids decorate cookies and cupcakes. Meal comes in an adorable lunch box. Package includes birthday cake.
☎ 01-398 574   www.cocoa-and-co.com

Cooking and Crafts by Special Events
Children are occupied with the challenge of preparing a three-course meal, including cotton candy and ice cream. Once their culinary creativity is satisfied, kids can make a stuffed animal, photo frame, or mirror at the craft stations.
☎ 01-861 700   03-864 971   www.specialeventsleb.com

Beauty

Girls of any age, anywhere enjoy spa treatments together, especially so in Beirut. So if the party is girls-only, a beauty theme is a safe bet.

Bella's Spa by Special Events
Beauty salon for little girls decorated in tones of pink and lavender. Offers fun facials, manicures, hair dos and make up.
🏠 Verdun, Verdun Plaza   ☎ 01-861 700

Spa-tacular
Hair and nail salon that caters to mothers and daughters. Offers birthday packages with onsite activity center and boutique.
🏠 Achrafieh, Sodeco Square   ☎ 01-397 702

Frizzy's Chez Lulu Spa and Salon

Salon targeting mothers and daughters, Frizzy's pampers little girls from head to toe. In addition to the standard menu of nail treatments, facials, hairdressing and makeup there's a fashion lounge where kids personalize beach bags – a fun idea for a birthday bash.

🏠 Verdun, Dunes Centre ☎ 01-801 601

Fast Food and Theme Chains

There are many reasons for avoiding fast food, but hey, just in case . . .

- **Burger King** 🏠 Raouché ☎ 01-802 948 ☎ Jal el Dib ☎ 04-710 827
- **McDonald's** 🏠 Badaro ☎ 01-386 773 ☎ Dora ☎ 01-891 891
- **Applebee's** 🏠 Dbayeh ☎ 04-541 222
- **Chili's** 🏠 Achrafieh ☎ 01-337 171 🏠 Gemmayze ☎ 01-571 157
- **Fuddrucker's** 🏠 Dbayeh ☎ 04-520 720
- **Hard Rock Café** 🏠 Ain Mreisseh ☎ 01-373 023

Pizza

A pizza party is always a great hit with kids, and Italian food in general is a popular dining out option with families.

- **Margherita** 🏠 Gemmayze ☎ 01- 560 480
- **Olio** 🏠 Gemmayze ☎ 01-563 939 ☎ Hamra ☎ 01-345 703
- **Aliacci** 🏠 Gemmayze ☎ 01-566 199
- **Napoletana** 🏠 Hamra ☎ 01-345 444 🏠 Achrafieh ☎ 01-332 002
- **The Peninsula** 🏠 Dbayeh ☎ 04- 540 240 🏠 Mtayleb ☎ 04-914 913
- **Olivo** 🏠 Bhamdoun ☎ 05-263 111

For a taste of Lebanese specialties, from kabab to manoushé, check out these popular local chains: Al Falamanki, Zaatar W Zeit, Diwan Sultan Brahim, Falafel Sahyoun, Kababji, Boubouffe . . .

Burgers

Burger joints are in vogue, and the competition works to the benefit of burger fans, e.g. teenagers. The best part about a burger party is that it makes accompanying parents feel like teenagers in love again.

Classic Burger Joint
Big bang for your buck. Delicious burger with best fries and bun in town. Atmosphere is casual, of course, with the beat of an authentic burger joint. The success of its first restaurant in Sodeco has resulted in the opening of branches in downtown, Jal el Dib and Zaitunay Bay.
🏠 Sodeco ☎ 01-444 050 🌐 www.classicburgerjoint.com

BRGR CO.
Gourmet burger place with a comfy, casual vibe serving Kobe burgers and Burgers of the Day. Fries, onion rings and dips are addictive, and the cheese cake dessert served in an old-fashioned ice cream cup is to die for. Special mini-burger packages work well for birthday parties.
🏠 Achrafieh ☎ 01-333 511 🌐 www.thebrgr.co

Let's Burger
As the first burger joint on the scene, Let's Burger started the burger craze. Here, it's build-your-own burger. The Swiss and mushroom burger is so thick and juicy you need a steak knife.
🏠 Achrafieh ☎ 01-215 888 🌐 www.let'sburger.com

Bob's Easy Diner
Casual, 1950s-themed franchise with tasty burgers and a varied menu. Any of the three locations – Verdun, ABC Achrafieh or City Mall – make a good location for a birthday party. Tell the kids to come dressed as a character from the movie *Grease*.
🏠 Verdun ☎ 01-860 111 🏠 ABC, Achrafieh ☎ 01-202 222 🏠 City Mall ☎ 01-886 986
🌐 www.bobseasydiner.com

Cinema

Sometimes the formula of a movie and a bite afterwards is just right for a laid-back birthday party, especially when the release is something everyone wants to see.

Empire Cinemas
- Verdun ☎ 01-792 123
- Sodeco ☎ 01-616 707
- Achrafieh ☎ 01-328 806
- Zouk ☎ 09-212 516
- Sin el Fil ☎ 01-485 590

Grand Cinemas
- Concorde ☎ 01-343 143
- Achrafieh ☎ 01-209 208
- Dbayeh ☎ 04-444 650
- Saida ☎ 07-723 026
- Enfeh ☎ 06-540 970

> **Gotta love Lebanon: the perk of advance reserved seating by phone almost makes up for the ringing of phones during the movie.**

Dress-up

Doesn't a little boy with a Superman cape in the supermarket melt your heart? Because we've yet to meet a little kid who doesn't like to dress up, this kind of party works well for kids and parents alike.

Darine Semaan
Darine does face-painting and performs art demonstrations for social events. Minimum of two hours and ten persons.
📠 03-388 547   🌐 www.darinesemaan.com

Frizzy
Frizzy offers packages that include costumes, entertainment and animation. Their venue, an entertainment and education center has activity corners such as Just for Boys and My Space, a crazy science lab with snow machines. The Beirut branch is located in Minus 2 at the Verdun Centre.
🏠 Beirut ☎ 01-801 601   🌐 www.myfrizzy.com

Doll Salon by Special Events

Salon stocked with dolls, accessories and clothing where children can play. Dedicated area for jewelry-making.

🏠 Verdun, Verdun Plaza 2 ☎ 01- 861 700

> **A word about birthday party etiquette:** When your child is invited to a birthday party, be sure to RSVP. Many Lebanese don't, and yet show up anyway, which is disrespectful to the hostess. Also take note that many parents (usually the ones who don't RSVP) bring along nannies and even the invited guest's younger siblings! It is acceptable to specify "No nannies please" on the invitation card.

Party Favors:

Little Things 🏠 Hamra 📱 71-959 528

Celebrations 🏠 Mar Elias 📱 03-422 010

Fiesta Balloons 🏠 Koraytem ☎ 01-862 683

Sparks Balloons 🏠 Koraytem ☎ 01-861 186

Cadeau de Retour 🏠 Antelias ☎ 04-521 280

You're going to love the hand-crafted, custom-made souvenirs for birthdays and other events by **Atelier Roula Bazerji** 🏠 Achrafieh 📱 03-652 888

Nayla Audi's Oslo

For top notch, artisanal ice cream you need go no further than Oslo in Mar Mikaël. Dessert diva Nayla Audi purveys the best ingredients to make original flavors such as rose loukoum, cardamom, chocolate halva, cinnamon, jasmine and pure lemon sorbet. Audi also makes heavenly desserts such as green tea cookies and madeleines, but for a refined twist on the birthday cake classics, try her Devil's Food cake with Smarties or giant Oreo cookies. Shop online and order in advance for home delivery. Oslo plans to open a neighbourhood ice cream shop in late 2012.

🏠 Mar Mikaël, Madrid street ☎ 01-576 464 📱 03-369 313
🌐 www.osloicecream.com

Angel food cake, delicately rose and delicious

Oreo cookies bring back sweet memories of childhood

"Beirut a thousand times buried, a thousand times risen." **Nadia Tueni**

Beirut & Beyond

*B*lah, *blah, blah...* What cliché haven't you heard about Beirut itself, from its having been the pre-1975 Paris of the Middle East-turned-civil war wasteland to sphinx arising from the ashes? None do the capital city any justice when it comes to planning a day trip. In brief, the city center offers archeological ruins and a cultural history that is easy to explore. As for the outlying regions, descriptions defy clichés but are hard to come by. What lies beyond city borders? Hills studded with pines, silvery-blue olive groves, snow-capped cedars and people that embody the Good Earth. Many villages are unique and well worth visiting. Following are surefire ideas of things to see both in the city and beyond it. *Yalla!* Load the kids in the car, pack *lebneh* and cucumber sandwiches but always leave room for a restaurant lunch.

BEIRUT

The Heritage Trail

In the works is a long-overdue historical walking trail with brass medallions set in the sidewalk and information panels in Arabic, English and French. An accompanying illustrated map will facilitate independent exploration of all the major downtown places of interest. The starting point will be the Beirut City History Museum in the ancient Tell area, but until it`s built the trail will begin at the Beirut Souks. Pedestrians will walk through the 2,500-year-old street grid, taking in the Phoenician Persian Quarter, several Byzantine mosaics and the restored Ibn Iraq and Majdiya Mosques. The trail continues past Amir Munzir Mosque onto the ancient Roman Baths and Gardens beside three vestiges of the Ottoman era: the Grande Serail, the Council of Development and Reconstruction (CDR) offices and the Clock Tower. Then it`s on to Riad el Solh Square past the Grande Theater and the Saint George Maronite Cathedral to the south end of Maarad Street, adorned with Roman-style columns. Here the unmistakable Mohammed el Amin Mosque towers over the block with its Ottoman-style minarets and bright blue dome, a throwback to the Blue Mosque in Istanbul. Walk on to the popular Nejmeh Square and you'll be facing the Parliament building as well as the adjacent cathedrals of Saint George Orthodox and Saint Elie Greek Catholic. Next will be the long-awaited Garden of Forgiveness integrated into an existing archeological site. Near here lies an ancient shrine to the Virgin Mary, the Nouriya Chapel, and the El Omari Mosque built on the remains of a Byzantine church. Go past the Beirut Municipality building and follow the trail down to Martyrs' Square. Adjacent to this square is the Canaanite Tell and the future site of the Beirut City History Museum. From here you can see Beirut's ancient harbor. This walk promises to highlight the layers of civilization that make Beirut so interesting.

Zaitunay Bay

Across the street from the Four Seasons Hotel and extending to the storied Saint George Hotel is Beirut's new prime waterfront marina with shop- and-restaurant-lined boardwalk.

New Waterfront

Just east of Zaitunay Bay, this waterfront extension of Beirut City Center lies on reclaimed land that extends the city's shoreline by 3.5km. A walkway built to defend the city from tsunamis affords picturesque views of the mountains across the bay. This area is currently surrounded by empty plots of land, so it's great for walking and riding bikes. Beirut by Bike and Segways have outposts and Kidzmania is slated to open here. Families should enjoy the New Waterfront before it gives way to the cranes and construction sites of real estate development. The good news is that a park is planned for this area. Let's keep our fingers crossed that the park is not sold out for yet another building.

BEYOND

Mountain Towns

From red-tiled roofs to olive trees and pomegranate syrup, each town has its own special history, products and distinctions. Here are just a few special mountain villages we love to visit.

Aley, Baskinta, Beiteddine, Beit Mery, Bikfaya, Bhamdoun, Hammana, Broummana, Deir el Qamar, Dhour el Choueir, Douma, Harissa, Hassroun, Hermel, Jezzine, Koura . . .

Coastal Cities

Byblos

A top contender for the title of "oldest continuously-inhabited city in the world", Byblos dates back over 7,000 years, originally as a small, Neolithic fishing community settled on the shore. Byblos is also, famously, the birthplace of the script that is the precursor of our modern alphabet. At the old harbor, sheltered from the sea by a rocky headland you'll find charming fish restaurants serving the catch of the day. Nearby are the excavated remains of the ancient city, the Crusader Castle, churches and an old market area. Today the cobble stone streets of the souks are lined with souvenir stalls, boutiques and cafés.

Tyre

An island in Phoenician times, Tyre was a wealthy coastal city with far-reaching colonies and a prosperous murex dye trade. Not only did the city attract Babylonian King Nebuchadnezzar and Alexander the Great, it is the birthplace of Europe's namesake, Princess Europa. With five millennia of history, Tyre has many important monuments and ruins. There are three interesting areas to explore:

The Hippodrome and Necropolis date to the 2nd century AD. Follow the Byzantine paved road to discover an extensive ancient cemetery, a three-bay monumental arch and one of the largest Roman hippodromes ever found.

The second area, located on what used to be island in the time of Alexander the Great is now a district of civic buildings, a mosaic road paved during the Roman period, public baths and a rectangular sport arena built in the 1st century. This arena is the only rectangular one in the world!

The third area contains Tyre's major attraction, the Crusader Fortress, as well as a network of Romano-Byzantine roads.

Saida

Saida`s southern charm is often overshadowed by occupation and conflict (international guide books warn to keep clear of land mines) but in ancient times it was an important Phoenician commercial center with trading links to Egypt. Ancient residents traded the famous purple murex and excelled in ship building, but modern visitors will find the Soap Museum, a souk, a hammam, the Khan el Franj caravanserai (ancient inn for horseback travelers), the Castle of St. Louis, the Great Mosque, Bab es-Saray Mosque and the Citadel at Sea. Don't miss the city's signature sweets.

Tripoli

Lebanon's second city dates to the 9th century BC when the Phoenicians established a small port in the El Mina area. The city has a colorful history that includes domination by Persians, Romans Muslim Arabs, Mamluks and Crusaders as well as destruction by earthquake and tidal wave. The city has a different feel and many interesting sights. Over 45 buildings, some dating to the 14th century, have been registered as historical sights. There are mosques, madrassas and secular buildings that include a hammam. The Khan el Franj caravanserai and the souks remain authentic and evoke an exotic atmosphere. The locally-produced olive oil soap is famous, but it`s the sweets that are worth the trip. While there, see Rabbit Island, the nature reserve.

Archeological superstar Baalbek is a temple complex standing atop a high point in the Bekaa Valley. The road to Baalbek overlooks the vast Bekaa, the ancient "Breadbasket of the Roman Empire." Before the Romans conquered the site to build the Temple of Jupiter, even before the Phoenicians constructed their temple to Baal, there stood at Baalbek the largest stone block structure in the world. A wonder to ponder with the kids is how the massive foundations stones beneath the Temple of Jupiter got there. Even archeologists can't figure it out.

A typical mountain village with red-tiled roofs

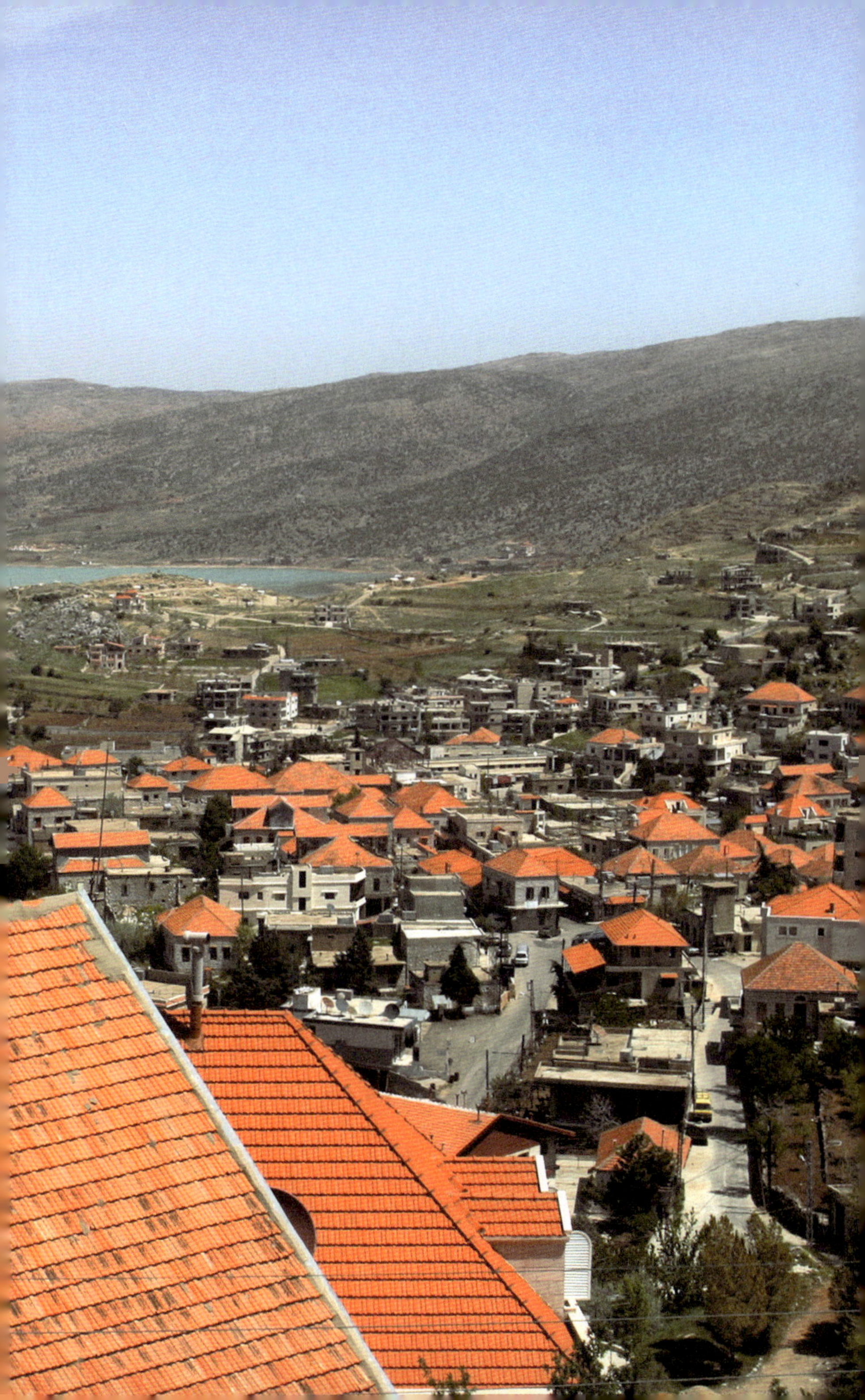

Lebanon's World Heritage Sites

Lebanon has five UNESCO designated sites of "outstanding cultural or natural importance to the common heritage of humanity." In other words, the following destinations are safe bets for a family day trip: Anjar, Baalbek, Byblos, the Cedar Forest, Qadisha Valley and Tyre.

www.unesco.org

Qadisha Valley

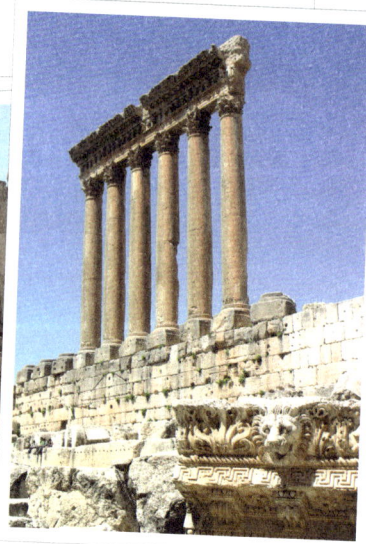

Baalbek

Anjar

Byblos

Tyre

Cedars of Lebanon

Getting the Gist of Beirut

Some things you gotta explain to the kids:

- You can learn to distinguish fireworks from rocket fire
- People "miss call" to conserve their phone units
- Car honking is a language
- Flushing toilet paper clogs the plumbing
- Hairdressing is mostly a man's job
- Just because roasted garlic (toum) looks like mashed potato doesn't mean it tastes like it
- Parents call their kids multiple times a day no matter how old they are
- Super Night Clubs are actually strip joints
- Taking photos of even the most innocuous subjects can draw the ire of soldiers and security guards
- Starbucks has valet parking and McDonald's delivers
- You may well find smokers in the non-smoking section
- Powdered milk brand Klim is "milk" spelled backwards
- The Electricité du Liban sign doesn't light up properly
- Even though Lebanon has 15 rivers and is located near the sea we have to buy water for our showers
- Yes, the guy coming the wrong way down a one-way street will get angry if you don't make way

Are you loving Lebanon yet?

About the Author

A Brooklynite turned Beiruti, Joanne is an honorary recipient of the Middle East Book Award as co-author of *Lebanon A to Z: A Middle Eastern Mosaic*. When she's not writing or editing, Joanne escapes to the Greek Isles to watch the sun set with a good book in her lap.

Coupon Culture

cookie dough
Luxury for Little Ones

20% OFF

Visiting Cookie Dough for the first time? Receive 20% off on your first purchase using this coupon!

cookie dough
Luxury for Little Ones

Maktabi Building, Mae Ziadeh Street, Clemenceau, Beirut   01-364 073
03-907 137   info@cookiedoughbeirut.com   www.cookiedoughbeirut.com

" **Cookie Dough** was founded out of an eye for **detail**, an instinct for **style**, and a **heart** for Little Ones!

Little Ones are as sweet and chunky as a ball of Cookie Dough and we think they deserve only **the very best!**

That's why we travel the world to bring them the finest and most **beautiful** pieces that we can find; **handpicked** from both internationally acclaimed brand names, as well as discreet upcoming designers.

We cater to your Little One's every desire; from clothing, **accessories** and **gadgets** to **furniture** and services; including **interior design** and **baby registries.**"

• Coupon cannot be used with other offers and promotions • Only 1 coupon per person

Spring Summer 2012

early learning centre

ELC Verdun, Abdullah Mashnouk Str., Tel: +961 1 793100 - ELC Achrafieh, ABC Mall - Level 2, Tel: +961 1 338040
ELC Dbayeh, ABC Mall - Kidsville, Tel: +961 4 444221 - ELC City Mall, Dora, Tel: +961 1 888499

15% OFF

Holder of the voucher will benefit of 15% discount at all ELC stores.

- Abdallah Mashnouk, Verdun, Beirut ☎ +961 1 793100
- ABC store, Level 2, Achrafieh, Beirut ☎ +961 1 338040
- ABC Mall, Kidsville, Dbayeh ☎ +961 4 444221
- City Mall, Dora, Beirut ☎ +961 1 888499
- www.elclebanon.com

more than a toy shop

ELC

Name: ....

Address: ....

Telephone: ....

Store: ....

www.elclebanon.com